John A. Wright

People and Preachers

In the Methodist Episcopal Church

John A. Wright

People and Preachers
In the Methodist Episcopal Church

ISBN/EAN: 9783337121020

Printed in Europe, USA, Canada, Australia, Japan

Cover: Foto ©Lupo / pixelio.de

More available books at **www.hansebooks.com**

PEOPLE AND PREACHERS

IN THE

METHODIST EPISCOPAL CHURCH

BY
A LAYMAN

PHILADELPHIA
J. B. LIPPINCOTT COMPANY
1886

PREFACE.

THE best argument in defence of the propriety of the following pages is to be found in the importance of the questions discussed therein.

It was thought that an analysis of the polity of the Methodist Episcopal Church would show that, with the lapse of time and the presence of new conditions, some of the leading provisions of its organization could be profitably changed and others enlarged to secure the more complete and successful use of the piety, talents, gracious gifts, and the means of the whole membership of the church; that as Christ has opened to the church more fields of usefulness at home and abroad, it becomes its duty to so adjust its forces that it may meet its increased responsibilities and do the best work for His cause; that as the work of man increases in importance and breadth with his age, so the Methodist Episcopal Church has grown, developed, and has now acquired all the powers that give a church efficiency. It has passed its formative state and needs to enter on its life of manhood; it must strengthen every muscle by exercise, employ all the arts that will develop its body and brain; must be clothed with the garments of righteousness, and do valiant work for the Master.

To do its full duty it is necessary that such alteration shall be made in its organization that the burdens may not be unequally borne, that each member shall contribute of his strength, so that the highest and best product of the united efforts of the ministry and laity shall be secured as the result.

To do this effectively all questions of class, caste, and rank must be thrown aside. The principle of leadership in the Christian Church is consistent with the equality of believers.

It was also thought that some such paper was desirable in order to call the attention of the laity to the connection of the proposed changes in the polity of the church with the question of lay representation, and to prepare the minds of the ministry and laity for definite and favorable legislation by the General Conference of 1888.

The world's history will have to be rewritten if it does not point to the end of the anomalous and incongruous connection between the power of the ministry and the obedient place of the laity in the Methodist Episcopal Church on the one hand, and the democratic government of Christ, the head of the church, and the equality of "the believers" on the other. It cannot be that in this country Protestants can continue to sustain an organization that so ignores its membership that not one lay member out of nearly two millions has the right or power in him or herself to vote on or to influence the polity or the administration of the church.

An objection will be made to the exposition of the dangers that threaten Methodism, on the ground that only the weak and vulnerable places have been exposed, while the strong points in the polity and workings of the church have not been fully set forth. If the objection is valid as to the latter part, then, once for all, let it be said that it has been held in view at every proper time to exalt the church, its ministry, and its laity as a whole, and to give it the fullest credit for what it has accomplished for the cause of Jesus Christ. That the church has done all that it might and should have done will be claimed by no one; that it would have done more if a more intelligent and unselfish spirit had been displayed by the ministry in the past is the belief of many of its most devoted members in the clerical and lay ranks. The strong points will take care of themselves; the danger is in the imprudent neglect of the weak points.

The object of this paper was not to praise the church, but to make suggestions whereby its usefulness could be increased, to give warning of present and approaching dangers, and to point out the way of safety.

Another thought will occasion an expression of regret in the heart of every true lover of the church, which is, that the General Conference in May, 1884, failed to appreciate the grandeur, the nobility, and the propriety there would have been in that centennial year in proclaiming liberty to its people, that in after-ages they might have had their jubilee, their day of deliverance to celebrate. Are the laity of the Methodist Episcopal Church inferior in their natural and scriptural rights to the Jews, to the slaves of Rome, to the serfs of Russia, of England, and of France, or to the slaves of Hayti and of these United States?

This question the ministry must answer, for they hold the keys which will loosen the shackles; the day of deliverance has been put off, but it must and will come.

The forbearance and patience of the laity have been sadly tried by the loss of the opportunity that such deliverance from ministerial control would have afforded them, to erect monuments of their giving in all parts of the country, for all the interests of the church. It requires the courage of a self-assumed superiority now to ask such contributions from a people whose dearest rights were denied them by the General Conference of 1884, and who are not considered worthy or competent to control the use of the contributions they are asked to make.

Finally, the reader will frequently meet in these pages a repetition of the same thought, argument, and perhaps, illustration: this the writer has not been careful to avoid; and while such repetition may be considered as in bad taste, yet it may be productive of better results by the impression made.

For the views here expressed the writer is alone responsible. They may or may not meet the approbation of many of the laity or of many of the ministry. The writer is willing to abide the results of four years more of thorough investigation of the subject.

JOHN A. WRIGHT.

PHILADELPHIA, 1885.

CONTENTS.

	PAGE
INTRODUCTION	13

CHAPTER I.

THE RISE OF METHODISM, ITS RELATION TO OTHER
    CHURCHES, AND THE CAUSES OF ITS SUCCESS 17
The growth of the Christian Church 19
Its form of government 25
Causes of growth of the Methodist Episcopal Church .. 26
Growth of ministerial power therein 30

CHAPTER II.

THE DEFECTS IN THE ORGANIZATION AND IN THE REPRE-
    SENTATIVE BODIES OF THE METHODIST EPISCOPAL
    CHURCH, THE DANGERS ARISING THEREFROM TO THE
    MINISTRY AND TO THE MEMBERSHIP 37
Equality of believers, proper basis of church government . 39
Dangers to the church 47
    First. To its inner life 47
    Second. From its organization 51
The constitution of the legislative and executive bodies or
    councils of the church and their practical working. . 54
    I. The General Conference 54
        Its construction 54
        Basis of representation 59
        Œcumenical Methodism 68
        Who should be members 72
        Clerical members 73
        Lay members 83
        Division of Conference into two bodies 85

To meet every six years	88
As a deliberative body	88
The selection and election of officials	93
Changes suggested	97
II. The Annual Conference	99
Its construction	99
Who should be members	103
Lay representation	106
The "Restrictive Rules"	118
Changes suggested	122
Incorporation of Annual Conferences	122
III. The Quarterly Conference	128
Its construction	128
Changes suggested	130
Lay conventions	135
Local preachers and exhorters	136

CHAPTER III.

THE DEFECTS AND DANGERS ARISING FROM THE CONSTITUTION AND FORM OF MANAGEMENT OF THE CHARITABLE WORK OF THE CHURCH AND ITS PUBLISHING INTERESTS 141

1. The official charitable work of the church	141
Changes made by Act of General Conference of 1872 considered	142
Defects and dangers	146
Changes suggested	152
2. The publishing interests	155
Their use	158
Religious newspapers	167
Quarterly Review	177
Defects and dangers	180

CHAPTER IV.

THE INJURY THAT WILL RESULT TO THE CHURCH FROM TEMPTATIONS TO WHICH THE MINISTRY ARE SUBJECTED, WHICH, WHILE PERSONAL, YET HAVE AN

INFLUENCE ON THE CHURCH, AND ALSO FROM THE TENDENCY TO FORM ALLIANCES FOR SECURING INFLUENCE AND CONTROL FOR THEIR BENEFIT AS A CLASS OR PARTY 184
1. The ministry as a class or party 184
2. Political temptations and loss of aggressiveness . . 185
3. Unacceptable ministers 187
4. Secularization of the ministry 190
5. Methods of securing power through alliances of the ministry as a class 199
   a. By exclusion of laymen from church councils . . 201
   b. By attack on the power and influence of the bishops 203
   c. By use of the Annual Conference 217
   d. Through the system of transfers 219
   e. Through the presiding eldership 225
   f. Through the term of service 231
6. Colored statements 253
7. Power over the purse 254
8. By undue influence 255
9. Conference aid societies 257
10. Endowments 259

CHAPTER V.

THE DANGERS THAT THREATEN THE PEACE, PURITY, AND PROSPERITY OF THE METHODIST EPISCOPAL CHURCH FROM THE ABUSE OF THE REPRESENTATIVE POWER HELD BY THE COLORED CONFERENCES 262
The remedy 269

CHAPTER VI.

THE INFLUENCE OF A THOROUGH INTRODUCTION OF THE LAITY IN EVERY DEPARTMENT OF CHURCH LEGISLATION AND WORK, ON ITS PROSPERITY AND USEFULNESS, ON THE PIETY, EFFECTIVENESS, AND COMFORT OF THE MINISTRY, AND ON THE PIETY AND USEFULNESS OF THE LAITY 271

	PAGE
Division of labor and its results	274
Woman's Foreign Missionary Society	280

CHAPTER VII.

The Position of the Clerical and Lay Members of the Methodist Episcopal Church on the Question of increased Lay Representation 287
Of the ministry 288
Of the laity 290

CHAPTER VIII.

The Laws of other Churches on Lay Representation 293
Deductions therefrom 293
Memorandum of laws 295

CHAPTER IX.

Résumé of the Changes that are required in the Organization and Polity of the Methodist Episcopal Church to suit the Present Conditions that surround and affect its Usefulness 300
Basis of argument and fundamental principles 301
Proposed changes in the General Conference 303
Proposed changes in the Annual Conference 305
Proposed change as to "Restrictive Rules" 306
Proposed changes in the Quarterly Conference 306
Proposed changes in the General Conference Board and Societies 306
Proposed changes in the publishing interests 307
The colored and mixed Conferences 307
Harmony 309
How to secure the proposed changes 312

INTRODUCTION.

METHODISM is now an acknowledged power in Christendom. The Wesleyan Church and the Methodist Churches of the United States and of Canada have secured this position of influence, by the grace of God, through the employment of certain means, coupled with a singular simplicity and purity in doctrine.

The Methodist Episcopal Church of this country, as one branch of Methodism, has developed into the largest of the family in numbers, in wealth, and probably in influence. The growth of Episcopal Methodism is among the remarkable facts in church history. It is the more remarkable in that its organization was an original conception, unlike anything in the history of church or of state.

The Methodist Episcopal Church has won its way so well and so rapidly because it has been a power for good. Its teachings and many of its peculiarities have been approved by thousands, indeed by millions, of people who have been and are yet in its fold; its influence has reached other Christian bodies and has modified their doctrines and customs. To study the inner life of such a body, to learn wherein lies its peculiar adaptation to the wants of man's nature, and the dangers that may lurk about its system, is a proper business for every one in any way interested in the progress of Christ's cause. No harm can come to such an organization without affecting all the churches, while its progress, growth, and increased usefulness will help and aid other churches in their work.

With the desire to impartially study the polity of the Methodist Episcopal Church, in relation to its present wants and its future usefulness, an effort will be made—

First: To establish the proper basis on which church organizations should be built and the scriptural relations of all parties to such church.

Second: To examine the organization of the Methodist Episcopal Church and the causes of its success.

Third: To show the dangers to which the Methodist Episcopal Church is now exposed. 1st. From changes in its inner life; 2d. From its organization; and, 3d. From the influence of the ministers as a class and as individuals.

Fourth: To suggest changes in its organization whereby, through the introduction of lay representatives in all its councils and by certain other modifications of its laws, these dangers may be lessened and the church be made more useful and efficient.

Fifth: To show how and wherein such changes in the organization would tend to increase the piety and usefulness both of the ministry and membership.

These propositions may be considered under the following headings:

First: The rise of Methodism, its relation to other churches, and the causes of its success.

Second: The defects in the organization and in the representative bodies of the Methodist Episcopal Church, and the dangers arising therefrom to the church as a body, to the ministry, and to the membership.

Third: The defects and dangers arising from the constitution and form of management of the charitable work of the church and of its publishing interests.

Fourth: The injury that may result to the church from temptations to which the ministry are subjected (which, while personal, yet have an influence on the church), and also from the tendency to form alliances for securing influence and control in the church for their benefit as a class or party.

Fifth: The dangers that threaten the peace, purity, and prosperity of the Methodist Episcopal Church from an abuse of the representative power held by the colored Conferences.

Sixth: The influence of a thorough introduction of the laity in every department of church legislation and work on its prosperity and usefulness, on the piety, effectiveness, and comfort of the ministry, and on the piety and usefulness of the laity.

Seventh: The position of the clerical and lay members of the Methodist Episcopal Church on the question of increased lay representation.

Eighth: The laws of other churches on lay representation.

Ninth: *Résumé* of the changes that are required in the organization and polity of the Methodist Episcopal Church to suit the present conditions that surround it and affect its usefulness.

PEOPLE AND PREACHERS

IN THE

METHODIST EPISCOPAL CHURCH.

CHAPTER I.

The rise of Methodism, its relation to other churches, and the causes of its success.

THE object of religious teaching is to gain access to man's spiritual nature that it may receive the training, development, and preparation which are required to secure, through His Son Jesus Christ, the fulfilment of the promises of the Father in this life and in the life to come.

The inducements that Christianity offers to man of improved health of body, of increased power of thought, of comprehension or grasp of mind, of a clean heart, of an enlightened conscience, of a purer life, of better relations with his fellow-men and a proper relation with God the Father, of Divine guidance, of support in trials, of a deeply-grounded peace, with the promise of perfect happiness in the future life, demand and should receive the most profound consideration of every intelligent being.

The measures by which these promises of God, the Father, through His Son, Jesus Christ, can be best brought to man are only second in importance to the fact of the promises. These promises, these teachings, affect man most nearly, for they define the laws that control the condition of his existence here and hereafter. To make these promises practical in the life of man, through them to bring men together and unite them in one bond and for one purpose,—their salvation and the glory of God,—to adopt measures for their promulgation among all peoples, embrace the leading duties of the church.

The tracing of the nature, character, and object of these teachings as they were first delivered to man, in the fact of his existence (being born with him), then the verbal communication between man and his Creator, by being brought face to face with God Himself or with His angels, and then as they came to man through His prophets, and lastly by His Son Jesus Christ, must impress on the student the conviction that there has been a constant development and unfolding of the Divine thought and plans toward man from the time of his creation.

The changes that have come during the past nearly nineteen hundred years in the teachings of the church established by Jesus Christ have been characterized by a law of development in the unfolding of great truths.

The simplicity of the teachings of Jesus Christ, of the methods adopted by Him for the extension of His kingdom, His failure to establish a church that should rival in its ceremonies the Jewish, which was to be put away, could scarcely be comprehended or appreciated by His disciples and followers; and while the truths the teachings contain are the same to-day as when delivered to man, yet they have in the time that has passed undergone many different interpretations. Yet it may be accepted that certain truths, or certain aspects of them, have been suited to man's condition at the time when they were prominent and had influence on his life. The natural tendency of the mind of man would be to take hold of such truths, or such aspects of them, as for the time seemed most important to his moral and spiritual welfare.

These have been given to man as he has developed the ability and intelligence to appreciate and accept them, and just as rapidly as they became necessary to the growth and development of his mental and moral nature.

The forms of worship and of the government of the church have been subject to many changes. The simple preaching of the gospel by Jesus Christ, by His disciples and apostles, soon degenerated into a seeking after the forms of the Jewish worship. Even the Apostles James and Peter looked upon the Church of Christ as but a modification of the old church in which they and their fathers had been reared. They could not with Paul and John cut loose from the ritual services of the temple; they could not readily understand the perfect liberty to which the disciples of Christ were called. Many Jewish Christians could not believe that Jesus Christ had come into the world to establish a new church; that while His teachings embodied all of the natural religion given to man, yet that in those teachings there was a new inspiration; that on His life and death was to be founded a new church, of which He was to be the corner-stone. The original simplicity of service and worship was not consonant with the character of man, and to it by degrees were added some of the Jewish ceremonies and Pagan rites of Rome and Greece. Man soon saw that there were elements of power and honor in the young church, and from many good intentions there developed the Roman Church as a spiritual power, and after a short time as a political power. The history of this church has been thoroughly written. The progress of man and the history of the Roman Church cannot be separated; it has lasted through all these centuries, and while its political influence has been lessened, yet it is a power to-day both spiritually and politically. To deny that it has, amidst all its errors, done much for man would be to deny his progress. For while much has been due to more recent protesting churches, yet when there was no other church during the time of the great invasions from the North, while governments were uprooted and Europe was in continual warfare, in spite of wicked popes, a debauched ministry, and a degenerate and deceived people, the Roman Church kept in its bosom the gospel of Christ, to be delivered to peoples in after-times who could separate the gold from its dross.

Wycliffe, Huss, Luther, Erasmus, Zwingle, and Calvin are illustrious among these religious alchemists, and while the separation was not perfect, yet in the formation of the Reformed Churches as a resultant of many years of struggle, such separation was well nigh complete.

But even then the same difficulties arose as in the time of the Apostles, and the result was the loss of the simplicity of the Reformed Church,—on the one side hankering after the forms, traditions, power, and loaves and fishes of the Roman Church, resulting in the formation of the Church of England, and on the other by the abandonment of the teachings of Christ as understood by Paul and John and running off into Calvinism with its doctrines so totally averse to the loving, tender, brotherly feeling and sympathies of Jesus Christ, thereby creating a church of stern, rigid doctrinaires, though with many characteristics that were commendable and worthy of imitation. The results of this division, or rather this breaking up of the Reformed Church, are plainly marked in the annals of the English and of the Scotch Churches, and in the moral character of the people. In due time, when man's necessity was the greatest, God sent that great teacher, John Wesley, into the world, and endowed him not only with the qualities of a teacher, but of a leader of men and a great organizer of the forces at his command. His education was solid, his acquirements large and varied, his heart and mind were honest, his purpose was single; and as the truth of the gospel was burned into his soul, so with his might and main he labored to preach that gospel to all people, and to gather his followers into a body that should be perfect in the simplicity of its organization and methods and yet be most effective in its work. Thus, without a consciousness of the fact, Mr. Wesley was the instrument under Christ of recreating and restoring, in the form of Methodism, the Reformed Church of England as the nearest approach to the Apostolic Church, in the purity of its doctrine, its simplicity, and its effectiveness.

Methodism was thus a special child of Providence. It approved itself to many who had found no haven of rest for their burdened souls, although eagerly seeking where one might be found; it met the wants of those who had but little of comfort in this world by holding up the Saviour's exhortations and promises of the rest of another world; to the weak in will-power it promised help and strength; it opened a large field of usefulness to many who perceived its spirit and its adaptation to meet man's greatest wants. It was an inspiration to many who had never before realized that Christ's invitation was to all men, that all might be saved and partake of His glory; that He would give to each one a witness that should satisfy him of his adoption into the family of God; that his heart should be filled with the love of Christ; that He had promised not to forsake him in this life nor in the dark passage, and finally would show to each one the Father in another life. Estimating these facts by the laws of human nature, it is no wonder that Methodism spread rapidly in England; that it gathered into its fold from all classes of society, and has been from that time onward a great spiritual power. Nor will it be surprising that it was transported into this country, where it could be freed from the entanglements which for many years beset, and even yet hinder its growth in England, in the overpowering influence of the Established Church, and in the stronghold which the Presbyterian Churches maintain over the

Northern mind. Its history in our own country, as well as in England, has been exhaustively written; it will not be repeated herein, except as it may touch the subject of this essay.

The preceding pages have been written mainly with the object of bringing to the attention of the members of the Methodist Episcopal Church in this country the proper place which their denomination occupies in the history and work of the general church, and to deduce from this position the further important fact that it has a philosophic as well as a moral right of existence, in that the general church of Jesus Christ on the earth may be divided into two classes: the one, the Catholic Churches, embracing the Greek and Roman, and the other, the Methodist Churches, representing the principles of the Reformed Church of England. With the former may be classed such churches or portions of churches that hold to the forms and traditions of the early Roman Church, with its Judaic and Pagan rites and ceremonies; to the latter may be added the various forms of Protestantism that, while spiritual and in the main orthodox, yet are narrower in their teachings, and hold certain special doctrines or retain certain forms which prevent the acceptance of the truths of the Gospel of Jesus Christ in their full simplicity and attendant power.

The character of the teaching of this gospel by Methodism has had a marked influence on that of other Protestant Churches, and some of their most thoughtful men are desirous of adopting many of the peculiarities of its methods and organization.

There is not space here to analyze the points of difference between these two great and representative churches, nor to compare them with those of their subordinate allies. As the leaders of Christendom they have many points of resemblance. Their methods of influencing men are based on an intelligent knowledge and appreciation of man's mental, moral, and spiritual nature. Each church directs its chief efforts in certain lines to reach certain parts of this composite being, man; and just as the special qualities of indulgence of the senses, of devotion, of reverence, of self-denial, of adoration, of imagination, of order, of fear, of duty, of trust, of love, and of awe are unduly or unequally developed, so will the person naturally incline to one or the other church or the branches thereof. A full and equal development of man's moral nature and intellectual capacity, under the teachings of Jesus Christ, would be perfection; it is this more equal development of the powers of the heart and mind that characterizes Methodism and has made her the leader of the Protestant Churches; it has also enabled her to divide with the Roman Catholic Church the honor of being the church for the masses of the people.

If this view of the position and work of the Methodist Churches in the United States is correct, then the responsibility on their membership is great; and if it be said, with one of old, Who can bear it? the answer may be, That all things under God are possible to those who put their trust in Him.

Such responsibility can only be met by a careful examination of the causes which have placed the church in such a position, and a thoughtful inquiry, to be made by each branch of Methodism, to ascertain if by any changes they may more fully perform their mission of spreading scriptural holiness over all the lands, and further to examine if there are any impediments or hindrances in the way. Before proceeding to make such suggested examinations and inquiries as they may affect the Methodist Episcopal Church, it is important to understand

THE GENERAL CHARACTERISTICS OF THE FORM OF GOVERNMENT OF THE CHRISTIAN CHURCH.

To do this in the fewest words, it may be said that the wisdom of Christ, in His knowledge of His disciples and the wants of His creatures, is evident from the fact that He gave no specific form of government; that He commissioned His disciples to go out into the world and teach the people His gospel, receiving support as they could, and when in need, to work at their trades for their own support; and that they might be entirely free for this work of teaching, the young church, in a mass meeting, directed that others should see to the poor and needy.

The most important meeting of the Apostles and believers that is recorded was called for the purpose of comparing notes and seeing if they could agree together as to the instructions of Christ on the points involved in the performance of their work. They met as equals.

The simplest idea, then, of a church is an assembly of believers in and followers of Jesus Christ, embracing men and women, "The multitude of them that believed." Some of these may be teachers, some caretakers of the poor, supplying the wants of the saints, but all are on an equality. From this form of government there may be divergencies for the purpose of increased efficiency without destruction of the cardinal principle of equality.

It is, then, by this test that the present organization of the Methodist Episcopal Church and any proposed changes should be tried: that if there are any provisions in its organization which are subversive of this principle, they are a hindrance to the cause and should be eliminated; or if any changes or additions can be made to increase the efficiency of the church which are in harmony with this principle of equality, they should be introduced into its organic laws.

CAUSES OF GROWTH OF THE METHODIST EPISCOPAL CHURCH.

The point is now reached when it may be profitable to analyze the chief causes of the growth of the Methodist Episcopal Church. This has been due (after the acknowledgment that all success comes from God) to the character of the doctrines preached by its teachers, viz.: repentance, free grace, the witness of the spirit, justification by faith, holiness of heart, and purity of life; to the active co-operation and employment of the laity in the religious exercises, to the deep spiritual experience of its teachers and people, to the earnest exhortations, the personal appeals, the godly lives of its members; to the hearty responses to sentiments that affected the heart or fired the imagination; to the whole-souled singing, the touching melodies, the religious fervor; to the earnest and trusting appeals to the Deity for help, and to the brotherly aid and sympathy. It has been religion on fire. The religious character and zeal of its ministry have added to its success: many of them were men of marked powers of mind; they were educated in a school that made few half-grown men. The frequent change of its ministers had great influence, giving the people the advantage not only of regular preaching, but secured to them a higher average of preaching than would otherwise have been possible, and has thus enabled the church to reach, by the use of the itinerancy and its system of circuits, every nook and corner of the land as it was opened to settlement. These pioneers, thus schooled, acquired a practical education that few men now have, and that is only possible in new countries. Among such men there was no room for gowns, formal services, written sermons, genuflections, bowing to the east, and so on; their work was more earnest; they could not so trifle with time or the interests of immortal souls; they had to be at work in their Master's vineyard.

The itinerant preacher, when his term of service was limited to two years, confined his teaching to a discussion of the leading topics in the religion of Jesus Christ, closing each sermon with a practical application and an appeal. This was strong food for the people; it was not diluted by being extended through a service of five, ten, or twenty years. Probably this kind of preaching was the stronger and the more pointed because of the inability of many of the ministers to present a diluted gospel in an attractive form. Their preaching partook more of the style of the utterances of Christ Himself, of the Apostles, and of the early disciples; it approached the yea, yea, and the nay, nay. The threatenings of the gospel were declared with deep earnestness and in tones of thunder: "Except ye repent, ye shall all likewise perish." And the entreaties and invitations of the gospel were uttered with hearts full of love for the perishing, with voices full of sympathetic tones, and often with tears: "Come unto me, all ye that are weary and heavy laden, and I will give you rest."

Such preaching forced its hearers to think and to act. That it had marvellous influence and power is to be expected from the working of the laws of man's mental and moral nature. Then, too, the condition of the public mind, the habits and surroundings of the people were favorable to the reception of the gospel as preached by the Methodist itinerants. Again, the personal interest felt by the members of the church in the conversion of their families, their friends, and neighbors, and for all with whom they came in contact,—following them up with their exhortations and with their prayers, rejoicing with them in their conversion and welcoming them into the church, had a great influence in adding to its numbers. This influence was continued by the watchful care over the new converts by the class-leaders. The encouragement to take part in religious meetings strengthened the ties that bound them to the church, for with these exercises came a feeling of greater personal interest and a sense of personal responsibility. These influences are of a higher grade than the social influences that also characterized the Methodist people,—

a result of their frequent association in the services of the church, the class- and prayer-meetings, the Sunday-school, and the benevolent work. Other churches may have a development of power from the social relations of their people, but they lack that special power which comes through a sympathy with the public and private struggles of penitents, the joy at their conversion, and the encouragement in their religious life, in the use of its special means of grace. These are among the most prominent elements of the growth of the church. To repeat: these are its doctrines, its means of grace, —the earnestness of its teachers, the efficiency of its organization, and the religious and social power developed in its people.

It will not be thought singular that such influences should have produced a peculiar people, with distinct marks by which their meetings are known all over the world; that there has been developed a certain spirit, a certain something that is felt wherever and whenever they are met; that this spirit pervades the people, and therefore one body is the type of all. By such a spirit Methodism is bound with cords that cannot be broken, whatever may be the divergencies needed to suit different conditions of time and place.

But while all this is true of Methodism, yet there are some points in its history and in the organization of the Methodist Episcopal Church that should in passing be noticed. It may be found that great as its progress has been, it should have or might have been more useful in its work if there had been certain modifications made years ago in its form of government.

GROWTH OF MINISTERIAL POWER.

To go back a short way in history. It will be remembered that when Methodism was first introduced into this country it partook largely of the character of its founder; it was his child, and with wonderful wisdom for the times, he gave not only Methodism in England its organization (effected after his death), but suggested that for this country.

As the church was started by ministers appointed by Mr. Wesley, and as they had to build up a people, it was natural that they should engraft upon the new church the principles of ministerial supremacy in which Mr. Wesley was educated, and on which he was forming the church in England, and that they should be influenced by the then prevailing doctrine in church and state: that power, concentrated in the hands of the few, was a primary condition for the efficiency of all governments. An argument in favor of such concentration of power was found in the fact that the ministers were more competent by intelligence and experience to formulate and conduct the business of a new church than the average of their members. It was also influenced by the time and expense necessarily involved in attending the meetings of the Annual Conferences (covering large sections of country), as well as the meetings of the General Conference, which were composed of delegates from all the Conferences. In the Presbyterian and Baptist Churches the same drawbacks of time and money did not exist, as the Presbyteries covered less territory, and the Baptist Churches were independent.

This cost of time and outlay of money could be ill afforded by the people. The support of the churches and the ministry, in addition to that of their families, kept the laity closely at work. How great such a demand of time and money would have been will be appreciated when it is remembered that in the early days there were no railways, few or no steamboats; stage-lines on only the important thoroughfares, the common roads imperfect, and transportation largely made on the saddle. The form of the general government as well as those of the different States were being discussed; there was a prevailing fear of too much freedom for the individual. Infidelity was the supporter of a so-called republicanism, and it was but natural that such facts should influence the character of the organization of a new church. The peculiarities in the organization of Episcopal Methodism and the distribution of power are, perhaps, more immediately due to the fact that its early ministers were evangelists, and that the form of the government of the church slowly crystallized on the basis of the most effective evangelistic work. Some of the earlier secessions from the church were due to an attempt to change this system to that of an established church, after the manner of other religious bodies. They failed both by reason of the inopportune time and because there was no generally felt necessity for the change. To harmoniously combine the demands of an established church with the evangelistic characteristics of Methodism is the important work of the present day.

The increase of the young church was most rapid

in the States south of Pennsylvania, among the middle and higher classes of people who had become planters. The travels of Asbury reveal many interesting facts as to the rapid spread of Methodism among this people. Methodism had in the South nearly an open field and was not hindered or embarrassed in its operations, except in part of the State of Virginia, by the overruling presence and influence of other churches. It therefore rapidly gained the ascendency in social position and influence, which it has retained until this day.

This scattered people, under these conditions, willingly accepted the form of government, the product of its evangelism.

The Methodist ministry led the emigrants into the West, and, except where they met an advanced emigration from New England or of the Scotch-Irish from Pennsylvania, the church has held the most influential place among the Protestant Churches. In the country north of Delaware, including New England, Methodism appealed to the humbler classes, the other Protestant Churches having the ascendency in society. Its churches were largely composed of Irish and English emigrants or their descendants, who in their early and home experience had been taught that to the ministry belonged the control of the church, and under the influence of such early education they acquiesced in the absorption of power by the ministers. The general acceptation of the form of government by the members was also due to the judicious action of the ministry in selecting among the members those best suited for class-leaders, stewards, trustees, local preachers, and exhorters, so that so far as the local church was affected there was no objection to the exercise of ministerial power.

The entire power of legislation in the Methodist Episcopal Church up to 1872 was thus in the hands of the preachers, and it was in accordance with the facts in the case when the Supreme Court of the United States a few years back decided that the Methodist Episcopal Church legally consisted of the bishops and ministers.

The Wesleyan Church in England was framed on the same principles, and its original and ultimate authority, "the hundred," is yet composed exclusively of ministers. That church suffered the loss of many of its ablest preachers and best laymen by its long-continued refusal to introduce laymen into its councils. It is hazarding but little to say that if at the time of the secession of the New Connection in 1793 a prudent yielding on this question had been made, other after-withdrawals would not have taken place; and to-day Wesleyan Methodism, in place of being largely a contributor to the Established Church of its richer members and of its talented sons in the ministry, would have held a more influential position, and would have been the means of doing more good as a united people than divided up as they have been and now are. The yielding of lay representation, although too late to remedy the evil that had been done, has nevertheless done much to establish that church in a stronger position; its collections have largely increased; new zeal in its mission work, church and school building has been developed, and the Wesleyan Church in England is made stronger and more influential by the admission of laymen into its councils, though with restricted powers.

The Methodist Episcopal Church in the United States has not been without its drawbacks in this direction. The secession of the Methodist Protestants, mainly on account of lay representation, gave the church much trouble at an early day. The separatists gained but little by going out of the church, except it may be the preservation of their self-respect. It would have been better for the cause of lay representation if they had remained, for by going out they not only did not help the cause of those who agreed with them, but hindered it for many years, by making possible the charge of disruptionists or destructionists against all who spoke or wrote in favor of introducing laymen into the councils of the church. The ministry were ready, as a class, to discourage every effort in this direction, and when the changes in the law were completed by the General Conference of 1872, they were limited to the admission in the General Conference of two lay members from each Annual Conference, adding in lieu of equal numbers the power of a separate vote. So much was granted by the ministry to appease the determined demand of the laity for some, although an unequal representation; it was yielded under pressure, and not by the free consent or with the good wishes of the ministry as a body; so hard is it for men to yield any portion of power once held or to divide it with those they have formerly ruled. They forget the fundamental principle of all government, that a grant of power may be for the benefit of a people under certain conditions, but when the conditions are changed the people have the right to resume such power.

It is a fair inference from the foregoing statements that the early success of the Methodist Episcopal Church was due, so far as its organization was involved, to its effectiveness, secured by placing the power in the hands of, at that time the most competent parties, the ministers. But as the conditions under which such organization was formed have changed, and as the new conditions now indicate the importance of a modification of this power, so the question comes up before the members of the church as to how much of the power, which is inherent in them, shall be withdrawn from the ministry by reason of changes in the conditions under which the church was originally organized. Among these changes, no one is so great or so important as the change in the ability of the laity to take part in its councils and perform their duty therein with credit to themselves and advantage to the church. The best evidence that the Methodist Episcopal Church is recognized by the Father above is in the character of her members. She can, with motherly pride, say, These are my children. There is now a large family, and they will compare favorably with their brethren in other churches in natural and acquired ability, in moral worth, and in religious character and zeal. Worldly success has been given them as a result of prudence, foresight, and industry; the good gifts of this world have been freely bestowed on them by a generous Father. They now have the education, piety, time, and means to devote to the interests of the church. With these changed conditions, the question that has so often been discussed comes up with greater force,— whether the laity of the Methodist Episcopal Church are as useful in the cause of Christ as they would be were they more freely admitted into the councils of the church, and made to bear a greater share of its responsibilities.

CHAPTER II.

The Defects in the Organization of the Methodist Episcopal Church and in its Representative Bodies, and the Dangers arising therefrom to the Church as a Body, to the Ministry, and to the Membership.

It may now be well to very frankly analyze the working of the organization of the Methodist Episcopal Church. It has been tenderly handled; the whole truth has not always been told; there has been a hesitation to expose its weak points, lest injury should result. The same arguments are used for keeping silence that politicians so well understand. This is all wrong; the Methodist Episcopal Church is too strong, too pure in its membership and ministry, to fear any fair statement of what may seem to some defects, or the discussion of any changes that may be suggested as improvements in her methods.

The action of the General Conferences of 1880 and 1884 must satisfy the members of the church that there is a decided unwillingness on the part of the ministers to increase lay representation in the General Conference to an equality in numbers with the ministers, or to introduce lay representation in the Annual Conferences.

The confidence of the laity in the wisdom of the ministry as a body was misplaced; the good results of the introduction of lay representation in the General Conference, in place of being, to many of them, an argument in favor of such increased representation, has had the contrary effect. The taking, in a few instances, of votes by orders; the instances of the independent action of the laymen as a body; and the failure of a majority of ministerial representatives to carry their points, has created a party who seem determined to resist any further introduction of laymen into the councils of the church. There is a prevailing fear among the members of this party that with the fuller introduction of laymen the influence of the ministry in the Conferences will be materially decreased.

The laity of the church cannot, then, depend on any free action of the majority of the ministry. Even the confidence placed in the wisdom of the ministers by the laymen was used against them, for the puerile argument was urged that such increased representation was not asked for, and this question, that should have been favorably decided, was referred to a committee, to report to the General Conference in 1888. In such manner were the laity of the church trifled with, and treated as grumbling children, and the interests of the church sacrificed that the ministry might have a few more years of power. Great leaders never wait to enact reforms until the people are in revolt, or become intensely excited and demand reform. An evil grows out of thus refusing reform in church matters that should be avoided, and that is, the suggestion of the question of the wisdom and single-mindedness of the ministry. Such questions will be raised when people feel oppression or any denial of rights. They do not stop to inquire very carefully into the reasons which actuate their rulers; they look at the end, and are apt to consider all who oppose them as wanting in some good qualities. Such conduct lessens the respect for and confidence in their spiritual leaders.

Great men should be the first to see the need of reform and prepare the people for it. This is what the General Conference should have done; they failed to do it; there is no hope in the future that they will act differently. The laity are thus forced to take action.

To help to a decision as to the policy and wisdom of introducing laymen into the councils of the Methodist Episcopal Church on terms of equality with the ministers, the following suggestions are submitted to the careful and prayerful consideration of the membership:

EQUALITY OF BELIEVERS THE PROPER BASIS OF A CHRISTIAN CHURCH.

FIRST: It is a prerequisite that the form of the organization of a Christian church should be in harmony with the principles on which the original church was established by Jesus Christ. To ascertain what such principles were it is only necessary to restate the substance of what has been already written,—that the church was made up of the family of believers, each one in all respects the equal of the other, and that as the numbers of believers increased, for the convenience of the body and to promote efficiency, certain duties were assigned to certain persons.

It will be well to remember, in this connection, that while legislative and executive powers are necessary to make an organization effective, yet the problem is to so distribute these powers that, while they secure the greatest wisdom and efficiency, they shall infringe to the least extent on the natural and social rights of man, and that they tend to help man upward in the path of progress. Knowledge, wisdom, and purity are required by the legislator; energy, tact, skill, and knowledge of men are as necessary to the executive officer. It is a well-established principle that in the distribution of these powers the liberties of the people, and their growth, the purity of churches, and their usefulness, are always conserved by limiting such grant of power to the necessities of each case. "Privileges," John Bright says, "everywhere tend to beget ignorance, selfishness, and arrogance." In this way, as nations and churches develop by wise legislation and the prudence of executive officials, less power of legislation and administration are required to be placed in the hands of the few: the intelligence and virtue of the people having increased, they can the better trust themselves with self-government. These principles are applicable to the Methodist Episcopal Church to-day.

Taken in connection with the principle of equality in Christ's Church, it is evident that a call to the ministry does not *per se* carry with it any power in the management of the church itself. Christ gave no power of government either to His Apostles or disciples. The call is to preach, not to control or govern the church. The ministers are to be the servants of the church, for Christ's sake. It is true there are some in our ministry who have higher notions of their position and of the extent of the call than Christ intended; there is a fascination for them in the Romish and Episcopal theories of priestly office, position, and power over the people, and they sometimes forget that Jesus Christ did away with a human priesthood. Many of them imagine that the laity were made to be governed by the ministry as some in past time argued that the black man was made to be a servant and a slave to the white. This idea of the priestly office crops out very often in the utterances of Methodist preachers. It seems to be imagined that in the laying on of hands they received the power to govern the church. An instance is at hand in an editorial of the *Philadelphia Methodist,* in the issue of May 17, 1884. In referring to the question before the General Conference, of the introduction of lay representation in the Annual Conferences, the editor uses these words: "Whatever the legislation on this subject, ministers will be in the future, as they have been in the past, practically the legislators and executive officers of the church, and why should they not be? It is pre-eminently their work, as overseers of God's heritage, and they ought to attend to it."

This is priestly arrogance; high-churchism without limitation; this is asserting the inherent right of the ministry to lord it over God's people as they please. It places the laity in the relation of slaves to their masters. This construction of the word "oversee" is not "to take care of the flock," "to feed the church of God," "to protect it from the grievous wolves," as Christ used the word. Jesus Christ is the great shepherd of the flock. "He leadeth them into green pastures and by still waters." The ministry of His church may have supervision of the flock; they may go in advance; more than this they cannot do.

The *Philadelphia Methodist* has many sympathizers among the ministers in the church in the thus strongly expressed belief.

If there is no scriptural basis for the sole government of the church by the ministry, and if the granting of power is for reasons of prudence and efficiency, then a ready test of all church organizations is provided. The first duty of the members (lay and clerical) of the Methodist Episcopal Church will, therefore, be to try its polity by these principles, first assuming to themselves all power in the church, and then delegating so much of it as can be properly used to make the church more useful and effective. How much will hereafter be considered. The point now is to establish the principles and to show where the original power in a church government is placed. That the power of the ministry in the Methodist Episcopal Church is nearly absolute, limited only by the small laiacal representation in the General Conference, was acknowledged in an editorial in the *Christian Advocate* of June, 1884, as follows: "We give our ministry a place of command, and protect the churches against tyranny." This opinion, so broadly expressed, should awaken deep concern in the mind and heart of every lay member. Though the fact has been well understood, yet its avowal at the time, in connection with the assumptions of the *Philadelphia Methodist,* has a meaning which will not be acceptable to the church. The laity will remember that a power that has to be guarded to prevent its tyrannical use is always dangerous to the liberties of a people; that there is a constant temptation to misuse or abuse such power, and that such abuse generally ends in oppression and revolution. The assumption of a divine right to govern nations by kingly power is not as full of danger to a people as the same assumption of a divine right given to the ministry to rule and "command" the church of Jesus Christ. The power to command in human governments is limited to absolute monarchies, such as Russia, Turkey, Abyssinia. Power in all barbarous and semi-barbarous nations is absolute.

The *Advocate* is in error when it says this power is so guarded that it cannot be tyrannically used. There is no limit in the Methodist Episcopal Church to the possible tyrannical use of power by a preacher or by a body of its preachers. They control every legislative and executive body in the church; they make the Quarterly Conference, can influence the election of lay delegates to the General Conference, are sole members of the Annual Conferences, and are largely in the majority in the General Conference. Every element of the power "to command" is in their control; there is no legal provision against the abuse of this power. Fortunately, the good sense and piety of the ministry have somewhat restrained an abuse of this power "to command." The laity of the Methodist Episcopal Church can never forget that the iron hand exists, though it be encased in a velvet glove. The existence of such a power is offensive to all right thinking men, for it suggests that of the king over his subjects, and of the czar over his serfs. Yet such power, according to the *Advocate*, is, by the organization of the Methodist Episcopal Church, in the hands of its ministry, and this without any legal restraints to prevent its tyrannical use. Methodist ministers should remember that Christ gave Apostles, prophets, evangelists, and teachers "for the perfecting of the saints, for the work of the ministry, and for the edifying of the body of Christ."

Then again, the institutions of a country, civil and religious, must partake of the general character and spirit of the government which accords them the right of existence. In monarchical governments power is given to the few, in republican governments it is the attribute of the many. The character of the government of the Methodist Episcopal Church by the clergy is therefore inimical to the settled policy of this country, and is repugnant to the feeling of its people; and while it is true that the divine government is superior to that of its creatures, yet the harmony and equality in authority in the church, established by Christ, are adapted to all governments and to all peoples. It may be reverently said that in leaving details of organization to the good judgment of His followers, His knowledge of the weakness of the ministers who would follow Him, and the peculiar temptations to which they would be exposed, forbade His placing power over His children in their hands.

History fails not in recording the fact that whenever man, under the garb of the priesthood, has succeeded in gaining authority over the church, sooner or later the result of the exercise of such power is written in the degradation of the church and in lasting injury to the people. The Methodist Episcopal Church with its glorious history cannot escape the same result if its future is left in charge of and under the control of its ministry. This statement may be startling to some, may be denied by others, but such denials do not change the history of the past, nor do they change the nature of man; the same results follow the same causes everywhere and in all times.

Again, it is not incumbent on the part of those who argue for the freer action and control of the Methodist Episcopal Church by its members, that they should prove that its success will be greater with such changes as the church at large may adopt. The onus of proof is on the other side; they must show that the unnatural division of responsibility as it now exists will more certainly secure success. The *prima-facie* inference is in favor of success by exercise of the natural rights of the people; it will take much reasoning to prove the contrary. To the eye of reason the ministerial power in the church is indefensible upon any principle accepted at the present day; there is absolutely no argument by which an arrangement which gives a man power over legislation, simply because he has been admitted into a Methodist Conference, can, in the abstract, be defended. The only plea to-day for the power of the ministry is, that notwithstanding its theoretical indefensibility it has worked well in practice; but this is begging the question. It does not prove that better results could not have been gained or that equally good results will continue.

The conclusion, then, must be, that all power rests in the body of the members, and that special power may be given for special purposes. There cannot be an Athenian democracy in a great church, there may be a well-balanced republicanism. On this basis, which is but a restatement of our former investigation, it is proposed to try the organization of the Methodist Episcopal Church as it now exists.

A single intimation remains to be recorded for the benefit of all concerned, namely, that the people of every country will have the use of their natural rights just as far as they are competent to use them without injury to themselves or to others. As civilization, the product of Christianity, is developed among any people will there be more liberty for the individual. It was but fifty-three years ago that the crown of England practically gave up its right to veto an act of Parliament; and in the recent contest over the extension of the franchise to admit more than two millions of the inhabitants of England to be voters and citizens, the House of Lords has been forced to bow to the will of the people, as represented in the House of Commons, and to forego its right of disagreement, when an act which affects the natural right of the people is passed by the lower house. The trend of the liberation of the individual and of the independence of the people is always to greater freedom and the enjoyment of their highest rights. As in the state, so in the church. The days of priestly rule are fast passing away; let the ministers of the Methodist Episcopal Church heed the facts.

DANGERS TO THE CHURCH.

The second important inquiry embraces an examination into, First: The nature and causes of the dangers that threaten the inner life of the church.

Second: The nature, causes, and operation of the dangers growing out of the organization of the church.

FIRST: AS TO DANGER TO THE INNER LIFE OF THE CHURCH.

Every thoughtful layman must be impressed with the fact that the Methodist Episcopal Church has reached a point in its history of supreme importance to the cause it represents. Nations, individuals, and churches reach critical points in their progress, when an error of judgment may interfere to stop their growth and destroy their prosperity. It seems to many that the Methodist Episcopal Church has entered upon its trying time and is exposed to injury in its usefulness from many classes of causes.

The dangers that threaten its inner life include the zeal, earnestness, devotion, self-denial, and piety of the ministry and members, and whatever may affect its religious character and influence on the world.

The Methodist Episcopal Church has done a great and good work for Christ. In the past, it was often looked down upon, ridiculed, its members treated as fanatics and its clergy rated as ignorant and ill-mannered upstarts. To-day Wesleyan Methodism influences the thought, the theology, the religious life, and the politics of England. It affects the policy of England in dealing with the nations of the earth. Its influence is felt wherever the flag of England is erected. The debt of gratitude due by this country to Wesleyan Methodism, through its immediate representative, the Rev. William Arthur, of London, in preventing the alliance of England with France in the early part of the late rebellion, has never been fully understood, properly presented, or appreciated by the American people.

To-day Methodism in the United States reaches through its ministry not less than one-fifth of the people of this country. The Methodist Episcopal Church, with its nearly two million of members, its twelve thousand ministers, with its churches, colleges, universities, and schools, reaches from seven to eight millions of the people. Its missionary work in foreign lands commands the respect, and often the aid, of their governments. It is recognized at home as well as abroad as a great harmonizer of social differences; as keeping close up with every forward movement of civilization; as being the best exponent of the truth of the doctrines it teaches.

Its ministers hold a high place in public estimation. Their utterances command respect. The laity are rapidly increasing in intelligence, influence, and wealth. They hold many of the highest places in the country, in the general and State governments, judicial and administrative. The union of the Methodist vote would determine any political canvass in the nation, and this whether for officers of the State or of the general government, and as its teaching is kept close within certain lines, so will the effect of such teaching be felt on all political questions wherein those teachings are favored or opposed. Mr. Calhoun felt the gain to his theory of secession by the unnecessary division of the church in 1844, and Mr. Lincoln recognized the power of this union of thought and purpose during the civil war. The influence of the leaders of the church is therefore eagerly sought by political partisans. The days of ostracism, of the refusal of public recognition, of the ministry and laity of the Methodist Episcopal Church are no more. In it there was little of danger, though it tended to limit the influence of the church for good. Persecution and neglect bear good as well as bad fruit. Rapid and marked success attracts flatterers, begets pride and self-confidence, and these precede downfall and disgrace.

The church is subject to the same laws as the individual. Nothing is so dangerous to a man as a very rapid gain in fortune or elevation in position or power. These tend to create over-confidence, to excite pride of thought. They make the man forget the steps which led him upward. So to the Methodist Episcopal Church, there is danger in her present numbers, wealth, and influence. All, if used aright, will tend to good, but if ill used, to evil.

Then, too, the tendency is strong, in the older portion of the church, to be satisfied with what it has done, to put on the dignity of successful old age, and to cease the vigorous efforts of the past. The respectability of its new position tempts to lifeless sermons and formal services. It affords a comfortable home to those who recognize that church attendance and membership are required by the customs and decencies of society. While to the laity these temptations may be strong, yet their greatest influence is on the pastors of the church. If they yield to these influences the laity must either follow in their steps, or by strong will-power resist such influences and save their leaders. If the church is faithful to her work, her future will be one of greater and wider usefulness than in any portion of her past history. If the contrary, she will decrease, and God will raise up another body to do her work. His work must be done.

The next possible danger to the inner life of the church lies in the failure to make such changes in its organization as will bring into active use all the members of its body. The human body can only be kept in a healthy condition by the exercise of its various parts. The best results of heart and mind are dependent on such use of all parts. So with the church. Its safety and usefulness depend on the full use of the graces and gifts bestowed on its laity and ministry, and its success is the sum total of these uses, expressed through its heart and thought.

There can be no difference in opinion among the readers of this paper that the church must carefully guard the entrance to her inner life, and keep out evil; that her future usefulness will depend on the continuance of the faithful use of the means and ways that brought her to her present position, under the favoring hand of the Head of the Church; that the church must freely use the talents, wisdom, means, and piety of her members. The church must not seek the things of the world, for they work destruction, but those of the spirit, which tend to salvation.

SECOND: DANGERS FROM ITS ORGANIZATION.

The organization of the Methodist Episcopal Church* is remarkable for its simplicity, for its completeness, for its efficiency, for the ease with which it can be carried on, and for its economy in cost. It is indeed remarkable for its covering of all important points in church life and work, and for its easy adaptation to all classes of people, in all countries. The intelligent people of this country, outside of the Methodist Episcopal Church, know but little about it. They note its growth, but have failed to understand the laws of its growth. In efficiency of organization it is in advance of all the Protestant Churches of the Old and New World, and surpassed only by the Roman Catholic Church. The readers of this essay will not need any detailed analysis of the organization. It will be enough to recall the principal points, that they may more readily understand, and appreciate, any comments that may be made.

Before the complete organization of the Methodist Episcopal Church at the Christmas Conference of 1784, the ministers appointed by Mr. Wesley had introduced

---

* The Methodist Episcopal Church South is included in all references to Episcopal Methodism.

the itinerancy, a reproduction of the evangelistic work of the Apostles and early disciples. The principles of the itinerancy so introduced were accepted by that Conference, and it has from that time been a prominent characteristic in the polity of the church. These principles were:

That the whole country was the field to be worked; that the ministry should be sent two by two, from time to time, to such places, and to do such work, as the bishop or superintendent should designate, receiving such support as the people to whom they were sent could or would give.

In place of having one Annual Conference for the whole church, the country for convenience of administration was divided into smaller Conferences, composed of the ministers residing at the time within certain limits. These met annually, that the ministers might receive their appointments, and that the spiritual wants of such districts of country might be more effectually canvassed and provided for.

The Conference territories were again subdivided into two or more districts, over which presiding elders were appointed.

In every circuit or station there was organized a body called a Quarterly Conference, with certain duties, to be held every three months, and to be presided over by one of the presiding elders.

The four points just named, viz.: the itinerancy, the law of support, the creation of Annual Conferences, and of Quarterly Conferences as helps in the executive work of the church, should be borne in mind, because efforts, hereafter to be noticed, are being made to alter their original status.

The only original body in the church is the General Conference, which is held every four years. It is the law-making power, limited only by the restrictive rules adopted in 1808. It elects the bishops, who are general superintendents, their duty being to preside at all meetings of the Annual Conferences, to assign each preacher, in good standing, to a charge in some Conference or mission; to watch carefully over the general interests of the church, and to preside over the meetings of the General Conference, but without right to speak or vote, because they are not members of the body.

The Conference itself is composed of delegates elected from the Annual Conferences, in certain proportion to the number of ministers, which it fixes from time to time, with one or two lay delegates from each Annual Conference. It quadrennially determines the boundaries of the Annual Conferences and may establish new Conferences. It elects the general officers of the church societies, editors of the church papers, and the book agents.

Such is the general organization of the Methodist Episcopal Church. It is indeed a system of wheels, which may be of iron, but are so wonderfully fitted that they work with great ease and little friction. Its system of question and answer, in conducting business in the Annual and Quarterly Conferences, is a marvel of accuracy in reaching details, avoiding disputes, simplifying work, and economizing time. No other association of men has so complete a system of procedure.

To an intelligent man a study of this system of the Methodist Episcopal Church must prove a pleasure and a profit. But like all other of man's devices there are serious points of defect, both in the theory and in the working of the organization.

It would be more than could be expected of any human institution if errors have not crept in and evils developed that need to be corrected, or if experience had not shown how to improve on the past. These points of danger, of error, of evil, and of proposed improvement in the organization deserve careful examination.

First: *The constitution of the legislative and executive bodies, or councils of the church, and their practical working.*

I. The General Conference.

This, as the central power, and from which all others derive their life, demands the closest study. Its general construction has been described. The changes that are required to make it more useful and effective are fundamental and protective in their nature.

The first point suggested for criticism is that it is, in the main, as it was originally intended to be, under the control of the ministry. The reasons why this was accepted by the young church have already been stated. While there was much that was objectionable to the laity in the power held by the ministry, yet the earnestness, simplicity, single-mindedness, and deeply-religious character of the fathers made many amends. Their government of the church was remarkable for its prudence, wisdom, and forbearance. But the construction and functions of this body now come before the people with different surroundings: *Primarily*, the members of the church can be trusted with the charge of its interests; they have the intelligence, appreciation of the doctrines and polity of the church, and the piety that has characterized the ministry. The membership is rich in men and women who have the time to give to church work, and the financial ability to bear its expense. *Secondly*, the conservative influences are now on the side of the laity; and, *Thirdly*, prelatical notions of power are melting away before a more intelligent understanding of the true position of the ministry of the church as established by its founder, Jesus Christ.

The basis on which the General Conference is constructed, as to its membership, is at variance with the principles already established for the government of a Christian church. The General Conference is not a democratic body; it does not represent "the body of believers." It is a ministerial aristocracy in the church. It represents the few. It was created by a class of men, by their assumption of power over the church. It has no authority in and of itself, as representing the Head of the Church; the authority of the church is in the body of believers.

If the General Conference were reconstructed in accordance with Christ's example, in harmony with the institutions of this country, so as to secure in its membership the largest amount of intelligence, wisdom, and piety, it should consist of representatives elected by the members of the church at large, both lay and clerical, without distinction of order; it would then represent the church. Such is the scriptural idea of the proper construction of the representative body of any church of Jesus Christ.

But the influence of habits, customs, and old laws is so strong that they cannot be at once changed, even when a better way is shown. Progress in the Old World, in the reform of government, of laws and social customs, is hindered by the force of these habits and customs,—the product of ages. It is hard to change inherited habits. We hold on to what was good in our fathers' time, or in our childhood; there is a fancied conservatism and respectability connected with them that is pleasant. In this New World we are less tied to old habits of thought; our very form of government is a protest against those of the Old World. The great changes in government and social laws are made by the younger men, before they have felt the force of the love for the old, and therefore, while the suggestion just made as to the proper and scriptural construction of the General Conference may not meet the approbation of the older members, its truthfulness and wisdom may find a lodgment in younger and freer minds, and at a future date may produce fruit.

The true theory of church government opens the way for a gradual change from the present unequal and unjust constitution of the General Conference in the direction of that which is better. It is therefore suggested that, while the proposed change might be considered too radical, a beginning in the right direction should be attempted by at least making an equal representation of clerical and lay members. The glaring inequality in the last General Conference will be seen by the following figures: Whole number of ministers, 12,628; number of clerical representatives, 263. Whole number of lay members, 1,769,534; number of lay representatives, 154. This makes an average of one ministerial delegate for every forty-eight ministers who are members of the Annual Conferences, and an average of one lay delegate for every eleven thousand four hundred and twenty-five members, making one member of an Annual Conference equal in represented power to two hundred and thirty-eight lay members of the church.

No one can give any good reason why there should be any such difference between the number of the representatives of the ministry and of the laity. The ministers are in no sense a superior order of beings. They are morally and religiously no worse and no better than the laity. They are not more intelligent; they have no greater interest at stake,—indeed, they have less interest, because on the laity devolve not only all the religious duties of the minister, except the teaching, but in addition the laymen have to provide the means for sustaining them and the church. Will the laity think of it that this ratio makes one minister the equivalent in influence of two hundred and thirty-eight (238) lay members; that is, the boy, with the down of youth upon his lip, is made equal in influence to two hundred and thirty-eight members of the church that recommended him to the Conference,—the wise fathers and godly mothers of the church. That one played-out minister, who is laid on the shelf for want of ability and probably of piety,—one who has tired of the work of his Master and has turned editor of a small paper, a travelling insurance agent, a patent-medicine dealer, a runner for newspapers,—is given, by the law of the church, as much influence by his vote as two hundred and thirty-eight of the best men and women of a church! Are the laity of the church prepared to submit to such a state of facts?

But why this difference? Why have the laity so long borne such things? Solely as a matter of habit. The church has been running in this groove from the first, and there is a disposition, natural enough with the ministers, to keep it there. The laity must wake up to the necessity of lifting the church out of this groove of inequality and injustice. In estimating the influence of the lay representatives in the General Conference, allowance should be made for the personal influence due to the larger number of the ministry; to the fact that the ministers are practised and skilled public speakers, have ready tongues, and understand how to persuade and carry the minds of their hearers. These two elements of power give the ministers, when added to their greater numbers, a decided advantage over the laity in a discussion. This advantage is increased by the presence of many laymen who were elected delegates by the management of the ministry, and by the presence of the colored laymen, whose votes were undoubtedly, in the last General Conference, under the control of a few ministers.

But the laymen labor under a still greater disadvantage in the fact that on the Standing Committees they are in the minority; the ministers greatly exceeding them in numbers. It is well known, also, that in all large bodies the preparatory work is done in committees, and that a majority report of a committee is generally adopted by the principal body. The practical result of this fact is, that the majority reports of committees, as prepared by and approved by the ministerial members, are usually adopted by the Conference. The sum of these disadvantages, under which the laity labor, reduces their influence in the General Conference much below that due to the proportion of numbers, and forms a sufficient reason why the representatives in that body should be composed of at least equal numbers of laymen and ministers.

BASIS OF REPRESENTATION.

With the change of the composition of the General Conference, by the admission of equal numbers of the ministers and laity, unjust as it may be to the laity, is involved the necessity of an alteration in the basis of representation of both orders. By the present law there is a great inequality; for example, the Discipline provides that each Annual Conference shall be entitled to one delegate for every forty-five members, and an additional delegate for every fraction of two-thirds of forty-five, and to two lay representatives, but that every Conference shall be entitled to one ministerial and one lay delegate. The unequal working of this scheme of representation will be more clearly seen in the following statements:

Basing the calculation on the number of ministers

and members of the church as given in the Discipline (1884) and the number of clerical (263) and lay (154) delegates who were elected to the General Conference in May, 1884, there were, First: 1 ministerial delegate for every 48 ministers; 1 lay delegate for every 10,297 members; 1 delegate for every 3830 members, clerical and lay members included.

Second: In twenty-four Conferences, each having less than 45 members, there were 772 ministers and 69,371 members, making 24 delegates of each order, or a total of 48. One ministerial delegate represented 32 ministers; 1 lay delegate represented 2890 members; 1 delegate represented 1401 members, clerical and lay included.

Third: If the representation of these twenty-four Conferences had been confined to the average number above stated of 1 in 48 ministers and 1 in 10,297 members, there would have been but 16 clerical and 9 lay delegates, or in all 25, or if based on an average of 3830, they would have been entitled to but 18 delegates. This inequality of representation, then, gave these twenty-four Conferences 8 clerical and 15 lay delegates more than they would have had on the basis of the general average, and 30 delegates more than if based on the whole number of ministers and members; being over seven per cent. of the whole number of delegates to the General Conference. In these twenty-four Conferences there were five with a total of 87 ministers and 10,582 members. They had 5 clerical and 5 lay delegates; one delegate for every 18 ministers and one for every 2116 members, 10 delegates for the

10,669 (clerical and lay members), or one delegate for every 1067 members. Thus these five Conferences had more than double the ratio as to ministerial delegates and nearly double as to lay delegates, and nearly four times the representation of the average of both ministry and laity.

Fourth: The absolute injustice in the inequality of representation will be more evident when a comparison is made with some of the larger and older Conferences.

The twenty-four Conferences, as stated, with 772 ministers and 69,371 members (total 70,143), had 48 delegates.

	Ministers.	Members.	
The Central Penna. Conf. has	209	36,908	
" South Kansas " "	95	12,203	
" Erie " "	192	20,202	
	496	69,313	
These 496 ministers and 69,313 members, together 69,809, had			16 delegates.

	Ministers.	Members.	
The East Ohio Conf. has	249	44,287	
" North Ohio " "	169	23,268	
	418	67,555	
These 418 ministers and 67,555 members, together 67,973, had			14 "

	Ministers.	Members.	
The Philadelphia Conf. has	259	45,976	
" New York East " "	248	45,181	
" Central German " "	118	12,326	
	625	103,483	
These 625 ministers and 103,483 members, together 104,108, had			19 "
			49 "

These figures show that the twenty-four Conferences, with 772 ministers and 69,371 members, making a total of 70,143, have within one of as many delegates to the General Conference as the eight Conferences named, with 1539 ministers and 240,351 members, making a total of 241,890; that is, with double the number of ministers and nearly four times the membership. This means that a native minister of Italy, India, China, Norway, Liberia, and of a colored home Conference has twice the voting power of the most enlightened and best men of any of the above Conferences, and that a native member of the church in Italy, India, Norway, Liberia, or one of the most ignorant in a Southern church, has nearly four times the voting power of the best layman of any of the Conferences named.

If the representation of these twenty-four Conferences had been based on the ratio of the eight they would have had but fourteen delegates, a difference of thirty-four.

Fifth: Nine of the foreign Conferences, with 21,577 members and ministers, had 18 delegates.

The Newark Conference with	34,550	members and ministers,
The New Jersey Conference with	35,346	" " "
The Central Pennsylvania Conference with	36,908	" " "
Total,	106,804,	had 18 delegates.
The New York East Conference with	45,181	members and ministers,
The Indiana Conference with	29,808	" " "
The South East Indiana Conference with	25,632	" " "
Total,	100,621,	had 18 delegates.

This statement shows that each member and minister in each one of these foreign mission Conferences had five times the representative influence in the General Conference that any member of the above-named Conferences had. If the representation was in proportion to members, these nine Conferences would not have had exceeding four (4) delegates in place of eighteen (18).

Sixth : Take the whole membership, including ministers, at 1,597,212, and delegates at 430 (Discipline, 1884), and each delegate would represent 3715 members, or one lay and one clerical delegate to represent 7430 members.

There are thirty-seven Conferences with less than 7430 members each, making an aggregate of 141,313 members. These Conferences have 86 delegates (43 clerical and 43 lay) ; each delegate representing 1644 members, or two delegates 3288 members. This leaves sixty-three Conferences having 1,455,899 members with 344 delegates (222 clerical and 122 lay), so that each delegate represents 4232 members, or two delegates 8464 members. This means that every member of the church in the thirty-seven Conferences (composed, in addition to the twenty-four foreign Conferences above noted, of all the weak white Conferences in the West and Northwest) has over two and a half times more representative power in the General Conference than a member of the older Conferences. If the representation of these thirty-seven Conferences was based on 4232 members, as it is in the sixty-three Conferences, their number of delegates would be 33, showing that they have 56 delegates in excess of a fair proportion. The excess of 56 delegates over and above an equal ratio is so large as to be wrong in principle, subversive of every idea of equal powers, and dangerous in its results.

It must be remembered that these differences in representation are not in favor of the larger and older Conferences, embracing the conservative as well as the progressive element, and including the numbers, intelligence, influence, and wealth of the church; nor in favor of the membership from which the support of the thirty-seven (37) Conferences is drawn, for, as already written, these are principally mission, foreign, and colored Conferences. In the face of these facts the General Conference has sent down to the Annual Conferences a proposed change in the Discipline, retaining and confirming this inequality by giving each Conference at least one ministerial and one lay delegate. The laity cannot too carefully examine into the results of such inequality and injustice. It is giving those least competent to judge the controlling power in the church. The fifty-six votes in excess of fair representation will decide any closely-contested question. They decided the election of at least two of the bishops and most of the officers chosen at the last General Conference. They can determine the policy of the church and change its laws.

Would any thoughtful and prudent statesman place such a power in the hands of a few? Would he give such power to the parties least in interest and least competent to make proper use of it? Would he not rather strengthen the power of the permanent and tried majority, of those who contribute the most, and on whom the church must depend for its efficient work? Such a policy as that now adopted in the Methodist Episcopal Church is at variance with the practice of all church bodies and of all civil governments. It is destructive of "all equality of right, equality of burdens, equality of powers, equality of privileges," that belong to all men in the church of God, as well as under the laws of constitutional governments. It is destructive of government.

Why should not the present law be changed and a just representation be secured to all? It is answered by some, and the plea was made in the last General Conference, that each Annual Conference is entitled to representation (lay and clerical) in the General Conference, and the composition of the United States Senate is appealed to as a conclusive argument. The first argument embraces one of the dangers to the church in the future, and will be hereinafter more fully discussed. The second argument of the analogy with the general government will not hold. That government is based on a union of independent States; their life is perpetual, their limits and boundaries are fixed. The general government cannot lessen the senatorial representation by change of State lines. The equal representation of the States in the Senate of the United States was, as is well known, a compromise to secure the union of the States. It works unequally and unjustly, but it is one of the inequalities in representation that must be accepted. The influence of time in the settlement of the country and the creation of new States tends to reduce its irregularity and injustice. On the other side, the Annual Conferences are the creation of the General Conference. Their legal life is but four years; at the end of that time their boundaries may be changed, they may be divided up and passed over to other Conferences, their existence and names may be extinguished. While Annual Conferences exist as part of the organization, yet there is no one Conference that has continuous life. Wherein, then, is there any ground of comparison with the principle of representation in the Senate of the United States? There is none. The Annual Conference is but a convenient, practicable arrangement for the transaction of part of the business of the General Conference representing the church. It is one of the striking examples of the executive wisdom of our fathers. There is, therefore, no justification for the unequal representation that is now the law of the church.

Finally, as to the right of representation by Conferences. It is asked in what sense are the delegates elected by the Annual Conferences representatives. Whom do they represent? In a legal sense they represent the ministers of the church as a whole, not those of a Conference. Theoretically, they represent the church. The election of the representatives by the Annual Conferences is but a convenient and practicable method of securing members of the General Conference. It has the same force as if the law made it the duty of every forty-five ministers in the church to meet and elect one of their number a delegate. It has nothing to do with any original or legal right of an Annual Conference to representation, and therefore there can be no claim, as a right, from any Annual Conference as such for representation in the General Conference. This exact status of the relation of the Annual to the General Conference should be understood by the church.

The same interpretation of the law holds good as to lay representation, with the important qualification that lay delegates represent the church, not the members of a Conference; that they, unlike the ministry, have the inherent right to representation, because they form the body of the church.

Further, the whole number of members, including the ministers, would give a more just basis for both lay and clerical representation in the General Conference than as it now is. This change would bring the representation a step nearer the true basis. It would look more like making the ministry, in a limited sense it is true, representatives of the membership. It would, at least, remove one of the evidences of the ministerial control of the church, as by the present law the number of the members forms no part of the basis on which the number of ministerial representatives is fixed. If this argument on the basis of representation is accepted, the adjustment of the number of delegates can be as readily made as in the present plan, with the exception that some way would have to be devised by which smaller Conferences and the lay conventions could unite in selection of their delegates.

If the Methodist Episcopal Church is to be the church of the people and not of the ministry, and if the representation of the ministry is to be continued, then the wisdom of basing the representation of both orders on the number of the membership must be conceded.

In connection with this subject of representation in the General Conference, it may be found necessary to undo the action of the General Conference of 1868, by which mission and foreign and colored Conferences were admitted on an equality with the other Annual Conferences into the General Conference. The next General Conference will have to look carefully at the influence which the representation of the colored and mixed Conferences, and of the foreign Conferences, has had and may have on her welfare. It may be found that there was too great haste in 1868, that the expectations of those who urged and carried this change have not only not been realized, but that the change threatens injury to the church. The influence of the representatives of the colored and mixed Conferences will be hereinafter considered.

The question of the influence of the full representation of foreign Conferences brings up that of so-called œcumenical Methodism. It is not proposed to discuss it any further than to suggest in advance the doubtfulness of the policy of admitting into the General Conference representatives from foreign Conferences, whether they may have been or are missionaries or are native converts, for the practical reason that while the doctrines of the church and the general principles of its organization may be and are suited to all peoples, yet there will and must be variation in details and in their application to the peculiarities and wants of each distinct nation. These variations will increase and will be developed in the growth of the church in such nations, and will ultimately assume a form of Methodism adapted to their circumstances and wants. As the wants of the members in foreign countries are brought before the General Conference through their representatives, these will be found to vary as they represent different peoples, and the legislation that may be asked for may be contrary to the wishes and interests of our own people. Such differences will practically unfit the representatives of foreign Conferences to legislate intelligently for the church in this country, and thus an incipient antagonism of interest and difference of opinion will be introduced into our councils. It is unwise to attempt the enforcement of any rigid form of church government on the membership in different countries. There must be an elasticity that will suit different conditions of the people. That these suggestions are not without force is proven by the fact that in the last General Conference there were nine foreign Conferences represented by eighteen delegates, and many of them able and influential men.

The conception of a Methodism which is to be worldwide is a beautiful and inspiring thought when properly construed. There is in Methodism, as has been said, a spirit, or a certain something, which is the product of its doctrinal teachings, its usages, its organization, and of its people, that may be transplanted with the church into all lands, and that will bear good fruit. But the expectation that the organization of the Methodist Episcopal Church can be profitably extended to embrace its adherents in all countries, without regard to numbers abroad or at home, will meet with disappointment. There is a limit to the power of all human governments; the leaders who have tried to make the peoples of various nations adopt their customs and laws, and become like their conquerors, have always failed. The same is true of the church: any such attempt of a successful church will break down by reason of its overgrown proportions at home, of its inability to harmonize the peculiar wants of all peoples by any human devices, and because its success among such peoples will most certainly induce independent action on their part.

The Roman Catholic Church is the most prominent instance of success in propagandism that the world has seen. It has had all the benefits of a history commencing shortly after the death of Christ; it has been part of the political and religious history of the world; it is founded on certain leading laws of man's nature; it too has a spirit, a something, that characterizes it wherever met with in the world. Its power of existence has been largely due to its political influence over its adherents; to this fact the governments of the world have had to give heed; yet with all its advantages, while the supremacy of the Pope as the head of the church is accepted, it is forced to assume certain characteristics of the mind, thought, and habits of the people of each country. But the power held by this church cannot and should not be repeated.

There cannot be a question that, with the growth of Methodism abroad, there will be developed a conviction that in many respects its polity cannot in justice to the home interests of the mother-church be changed to suit the needs of the churches in foreign lands. This feeling, with one of self-reliance, with the worthy ambition of native leaders, and the decided objection of all governments to the religious control of their people by foreign organizations, will, as rapidly as can be, cause these bodies to organize on their own basis and produce a Methodism suited to their circumstances and conditions. In place, then, of the Methodist Episcopal Church being spread over all the world, the time will come when there will be a Methodism of Japan, of China, of India, of Africa, of Germany, of Switzerland, of Sweden, of Denmark, of Mexico, of South America, and of all countries where our church may have had its greatest successes.

The same law will work at home, and as the membership increases it will meet a less migratory people, and as the people hold on to their homes there will be developed more striking differences among them in different parts of this country. So in time these differences will furnish a basis for different branches of the church. These may be founded on nationalities, on races; they may be the effect of climate, of employment, of trade. Indeed, there are many influences which will in the future mark most distinctively the inhabitants of different parts of this country; and yet with all these differences at home and abroad, and with the peculiar character of the churches that will arise, they will all have the distinctive spirit of Methodism, they will bear its features so strongly that they may not be mistaken. They will be children of one family, having a common lineage, and be partakers of the same inheritance. In this glorious future of the church there is cause for increased effort, for broad statesmanship, for a clear recognition of the object to be gained, and great care is needed that its work shall not be impeded or degraded either by unworthy ambition or by a narrow and defective policy.

A fair inference from this discussion is, that the policy of the church should not have been changed, as it was by the General Conference of 1868, in admitting the delegates of the foreign mission Conferences to the full rights of the representatives of the home Conferences. Their rights could be fully protected and their interests cared for by the presence of their delegates in the General Conference, with power to vote on questions affecting their mission work. A return to the policy of the church up to 1868 may prove to be the safest course, in view of the hastiness of the change made in 1868 and its results.

WHO SHOULD BE MEMBERS OF THE GENERAL CONFERENCE?

This is an important question. On a proper construction of that body depends the future of the church. To answer the question wisely would require a careful consideration of many points, some of which will be here discussed. It may be superfluous to say that the great aim in the selection of delegates should be to secure the men in both orders most noted for their intelligence, sound judgment, practical piety, and for their love of the church, its doctrines and usages. To secure such representatives, and to prevent the exercise of too great personal and official influence in the body, are problems in the state as well as in the church; various precautions have been made by both to meet the difficulty. The only provision against official influence in the

Methodist Episcopal Church is relative to the bishops, whose power in the General Conference is limited to presiding, without the right to take part in debate or to vote.

It may be that further guards should be placed around the General Conference to secure safety in its legislation. It may be necessary to prevent classes of men from being representatives who would naturally be influenced by the desire for office in the church,— for its honors or its emoluments, or for both,—or in whom there may be, from their position, a natural desire to control legislation or the elections, or to assume a self-assigned leadership, or who may be exposed to the temptation to make combinations among the delegates to secure their objects. Too much care cannot be used.

The dangers connected with this subject of representation may be further exemplified by considering two questions: First: Who should be eligible as ministerial representatives? One requisite will be conceded by all: they should be ministers engaged in full work. The second may not be so acceptable: the right of being a delegate should be limited to the travelling and effective ministers. They do the chief work of the ministry in the church; they are brought into direct contact with the members and the people of the country; they are constantly testing the adaptation of the organization to the wants of the church; they understand most thoroughly its workings; they bear the drawbacks and make the sacrifices which are part of the lot of a Methodist preacher; these men compose the ministerial army on which much of the growth and usefulness of the church depends. This army may require officers, but such officers should be so closely allied to the rank and file as to sympathize in their labors and privations, as well as in their successes. The connection must be most intimate. One reason for the success of the German army in the recent war with France is attributable to the fact that the officers and men of each division were taken from the same district of country and were not separated. They had a common bond in their home associations and folk-songs, as well as in their national pride. The result, then, of the position and work of the travelling ministers is that they are the better fitted to deliberate on all questions of changes, and as a sequence, that they are better prepared for the performance of their duties as representatives than other ministers can be who have not had the same preparation.

Having shown what class of the ministers are the best fitted for representatives in the General Conference, the examination of this question might be closed, but it may be better to proceed and give reasons why certain other classes of ministers should be excluded from being representatives in the General Conference.

The question will be asked, Who are comprised in these words "The travelling and effective ministry"? There will be no question as to including in this number those who, in the Annual Conferences, yearly receive their appointments as presiding elders or as preachers on a circuit, or are assigned to stations or to missions. It would exclude all others. The classes of the ministry that would be thus excluded are,—

First: All superannuated and supernumerary preachers attached to an Annual Conference.

Second: The secretaries of the Missionary, Church Extension, Freedmen's Aid, Education, Tract, and Sunday-School Boards, who are elected by the General Conference, and all appointees of the Annual Conferences other than the regular travelling ministers.

Third: The editors of the official papers and publications of the church, with the agents of the Book-Rooms.

Fourth: All educators (except professors in the Theological Seminaries), agents of societies, whether under the supervision of the Methodist Episcopal Church or not.

Some of the reasons for such exclusion may be given, as follows: The work of these excluded classes separates them from the inner and active life of the church; their work is general, and they lose their identity with the local churches; their home influence is decreased, while their general influence may be increased. These results multiply with their years of separation from the pastorate; they lose their adaptation to the work of pastors, and as a consequence rarely return to it. Official life is antagonistic to the chief business of a Methodist minister; it is not conducive to his spiritual growth, for want of the food the active work supplies in the regular preaching of the gospel, and in saving and guiding immortal souls. The admixture of the management of monetary matters with official duties generally decreases fervor and pulpit power,—in fine, official preachers lose many of the characteristics which so eminently fit the travelling ministry for the position of legislators of the church.

To exclude all the superannuated and supernumerary preachers as a class may seem to be very harsh, heartless, and unjust. To say that the brother who has served the church most faithfully for many years, and who holds a high and honored place in the affections of his brethren, shall not be a representative because of age or infirmity needs to be defended with very sound reasons. It is thought that these reasons may be found in the large number of ministers, who come under this class in the Annual Conferences, who are by common consent unworthy of and unfitted for being delegates, and in the safe general rule that they are not in the full and active work of the ministry, and therefore have no just claim to either the honor or duties of the Conference. The honors as well as the responsibilities belong fairly to those who bear the burdens.

The thoughtful among these brethren, and those who value the good of the church above their own interests, will accept the result; they know that special provision cannot be made for special cases, and that every human law bears harshly on some one. Then, too, they know that the right of being a delegate is of little value, for the younger and more energetic push their elders aside. They must recognize the fact that the progress of the church, as well as of the world, depends upon the younger men. There is one atom of comfort to these brethren, in that there may come a time when the laity can purge the lists of Conference members, and then the right of being a representative may be in some way restored to the most worthy, as a mark of honor.

The objection to a membership in a General Conference of the ministers of the second class is, of course, not to the brethren who now or who may hereafter hold these places, but it arises from their dual position as members of the body and as officials of the body, an incongruity in its very nature.

The presence of these officials in the General Conference has been defended by reference to the custom prevailing in the Parliaments, Assemblies, and Reichstags of the limited monarchies of the Old World, where the members of a ministry have a place; in some they have the right of membership by virtue of their office, and in others, as in England, they must be first elected by the people to the House of Commons. The parallel will not hold good. In the General Conference of the Methodist Episcopal Church the officials represent no crowned head, no aristocracy, no party; they prepare no measures of legislation by virtue of their office, and are not subject to a forced resignation by the will of a majority of the Conference. As delegates representing an Annual Conference they are on an equality with their fellow-members. The objection to their presence as members in the General Conference arises from the dangers that may result to the church from the undue use of their official influence.

If necessary, it would be an easy task to show wherein the presence of officials in representative bodies is regarded as an element of power in the hands of kings and emperors, and where, in more advanced constitutional governments, great care is taken to protect the people from the dangers arising from such presence.

The example of our own government furnishes what to loyal citizens should be a conclusive argument on this point, in the exclusion of the cabinet from membership in either the House or Senate of the United States.

As a general statement, the dangers to which a state or church is exposed by the presence of its official members in its legislative bodies are due to their greater personal influence; to the temptation to assume leadership, to control legislation, and to place their supporters in the various offices; to the fact that they act as judges of the performance of their official duties, and desire to perpetuate their power by securing a re-election. Human nature is much the same everywhere, and where no moral question is involved, the temptation to secure power, to retain and use it, is too much for the average of mankind to resist. But few men can use power successfully: it upsets their judgment, and great harm may be done before even the misuse of power by a bad or imprudent man can be corrected. The general acquaintance with and knowledge of the leading men in the different Conferences, through their official relations, gives a great advantage to ambitious officials in the Methodist Episcopal Church for the carrying out of their plans. They can form combinations and produce results without exposing themselves; they can make men and put them down, and they can prevent or hinder any undesirable inquiry into their official work; they never combine against the perpetuation of their own influence. The injurious and demoralizing tendencies of this list of probabilities can scarcely be overestimated. Selfishness and deceit seem to be necessary qualities of a great leader, and are as apt to be developed in leaders of churches as of civil governments. These dangers are inherent in the presence of officials in all corporations, societies, associations, churches, and civil governments; the most that can be done is to limit as far as possible their production. Our national government has excluded the cabinet of the President from its halls of legislation as a protective measure. The Methodist Episcopal Church should follow the wise example; where there is no temptation there is no sin.

It might even be intimated that the majority of deliberative bodies would feel relieved by the absence of the office-holders. They might feel that there was a fairer chance to get at the opinions and judgment of less aggressive and more modest men, and that important questions could be more fully and freely discussed. The seemingly inseparable union between officials and attempted leadership of representative bodies does not always tend to produce the best results.

The loss of the knowledge and counsel of these brethren that the General Conference may sustain by their exclusion might be partially made up by a provision that such representatives may have the right to a place on the floor of the house or on the platform to give such information as the Conference may desire as to the work of their respective boards.

The objection to the presence of members of the third and fourth classes is simply that they are not doing purely ministerial work, and all the objections that apply to the other classes are applicable to them. To be thus ostracised may seem hard, but these brethren are not forced to accept such places; it is their voluntary act. They need not be put in this position if they follow their proper calling; and if the church deems it to its interest that the lines of membership in General Conferences shall be closely drawn, they cannot reasonably object. There is force in the suggestion that their work can be as well done by laymen. How much this amounts to will be more fully explained in a future reference to certain offices; but the principle should be established in the Methodist Episcopal Church that nothing but the pure work of the ministry in preaching the gospel of Jesus Christ, as an exclusive life-work, should entitle any one to full relations with the Conferences. There is great danger to the church in so extending the range of what may be designated as proper ministerial work as to degrade the call to the ministry. In an earlier day there was a necessity for much of this divergence from the proper work of a minister; but it is now the duty of the church to limit such divergences as rapidly as the necessity ceases to exist. The distinct declaration by the church that the most honored men in the ministry are those engaged in the pastorate, and that its highest office (the place of bishop) was to be limited to such pastors, would do much to restrain the eager thirst for the highest, as well as for the subordinate, places.

A single suggestion remains to be named under this head,—namely, that much of the danger to which the church is exposed by the presence of officials in its highest council would be prevented by a law declaring the members of a General Conference ineligible to any official position in the church. The working of such a law would be easy to foretell; it would do much to prevent the electioneering and bargaining that is now done in the Annual and General Conferences.

In conclusion, it may be said that by such exclusion the church would deprive itself of the benefit of the counsel of many of its best minds and influential leaders. This may be, but the church will feel very thankful to its Great Head that He has provided so many men of this description that the absence of a dozen or twenty of them from the General Conference floor cannot seriously affect the required sum total of wisdom and piety. Their absence will develop many others through their increased responsibility and their freedom from official assumption of superior knowledge.

These suggestions as to the proper constitution of the General Conference are based on two reasons: First, That the active and efficient travelling ministers are the best judges of the wants of the church; and, Secondly, That the safety and purity of its chief council will be better conserved. But it is frankly acknowledged that in the present temper of the church such a radical change of policy is not practicable. There have been no restrictions of terms of membership in the General Conference in the past, and whatever changes can be made in the line of reform and protection must be by gradual steps. The official posts have been sought for as the places of honor and influence, as stepping-

f

stones to the episcopate. The educational interests of the church have had the care of some of the best and ablest ministers in the church: there has always existed a close connection between the ministry of all the churches and education, the church at large being the foster-mother of education. Ministers, distinguished as representative men, have held editorial chairs, have served the country as secretaries of the American and other Bible Societies, and have even been willing to accept the office of Book Agents. Physical infirmity may have overtaken men in the early years of their service, and forced them, with other reasons, to leave the active work and accept office. That all these classes can be deprived of their present right of being elected as delegates to the General Conference is out of the question, however desirable it might be. The present transition going on between supplying the official places, where the education and functions of the ministry are not required, with ministers or with laymen is not sufficiently defined or accepted by the church. This will come with time. Nor is the danger to the church, from the presence in the General Conference of ministers holding official and elective places, so apparent to either order that such measures can be now adopted. Until the church thoroughly comprehends the fact of danger, its near presence, and the necessity of protecting itself even to the extent that has been herein demonstrated, it will be argued, with some force, that such a change would be regarded as casting discredit upon the leading ministers of the church; that such a discrediting of the ministry would cripple the energies and lessen the ambition of the young; that it would be equivalent to disparaging high acquirements; that it would narrow the work of the ministry; that the ministry could not succeed with a suspicion thus cast upon them, that they were not to be trusted to legislate for the church. The weak points in these arguments are readily seen. They are, in fact, but apologies for personal recognition and possible honor.

As reforms to be successful must be gradual, without yielding the principle, and for prudential reasons, the recommendations may be modified by excluding from membership in the General Conference, First: The secretaries of the different boards, unless a future recommendation should be adopted that they be appointed by the managers thereof. They would then be purely executive officers of the boards, while the present arrangement makes them the superior officers and the function of the managers advisory only. Secondly: The supernumerary and superannuated members of an Annual Conference, for reasons already stated. Thirdly: The editors and Book Agents who may be members of an Annual Conference. The same law should apply to the laity in the event of their becoming secretaries, editors, or agents.

THE LAITY OF THE CHURCH.

Having answered the question of ministerial membership in the General Conference, the inquiry naturally follows, "Who are the laity, and how should they be represented?"

The question "Who compose the laity of the church?" would seem to be answered by saying that the laity consists of all the members (male and female) of the church who are not members of an Annual Conference. A moment's reflection, however, will show that this description places on the laity the load of carrying some who profess to be more than laymen. It includes the local preachers, and would also embrace all ministers who for a time might be excluded from the regular and effective ministry by reason of their semi-worldly occupations. The carrying of this extra load might prove a burden to the laity, as it might interfere, as the presence of local preachers in lay conventions has already done, with the free expression of the laymen in their choice of lay delegates. There might be some relief from this if all such ministers could be gathered into a third order and given a kind of suspended existence. But this is out of the question, and the laity will have meekly to bear their burdens and accept the description above given, that the term "laity" comprises all the members (male and female) of the Methodist Episcopal Church who are not members of an Annual Conference. From this body the delegates to the General Conference must be selected. There should be a provision that in the representation from a lay convention to a General Conference the ratio of local or other preachers shall not be more than one to three, four, five, or more of the laity, when there may be four, five, or more lay delegates elected. When there are less than three delegates, local or other preachers should not be chosen. The Methodist Episcopal Church South, and the colored

Methodist Episcopal Church, found it necessary to introduce a limitation by making the proportion one to four. A reason for increasing such ratios in the Methodist Episcopal Church can be found in the action taken by the National Society of Local Preachers to secure their recognition by the General Conference as an independent body with quite large powers.

Another important question is, Shall the delegates continue to meet in one or in two bodies? If equal representation is granted, and the delegates continue to meet as one body, the right to call for a separate vote should still be allowed either order. But there are many reasons that indicate the necessity of a separation, or some change that will avoid the dangers so plainly seen in the last General Conference, and that will secure positive advantages in the deliberations of the body, in the choice of bishops and officials, and in securing a conservative policy.

In all advanced governments, the presence of two legislative bodies is an accepted necessity to secure proper legislation; one of the bodies is generally composed of the immediate representatives of the people, the other body of members having hereditary rank, or of members holding their term of office for a length of time sufficient to pass through the life of any temporary excitement of the public mind. These arrangements secure careful legislation, save it from the influence of an unduly excited public opinion, give confidence to the people that there has been no undue haste in such legislation, insure greater respect for the laws and for the law-making powers, strengthen the government, and increase the well-being and well-doing of the people. The same reasoning is applicable to the Methodist Episcopal Church. The General Conference has now become a large, important, and influential body; to it is intrusted the religious guidance of many people; it exercises an important influence on the welfare of the country. The church ought not, in view of its responsibility to God, to neglect any provisions in its organization that will increase its usefulness; secure the best legislation, the purest and best fitted bishops and officials, and the greatest conservatism in policy.

The determination of the question of instituting two houses in the General Conference will depend on two points: First, The wisdom of the policy which has just been noticed; and, Second, The construction of these bodies. In the Episcopal Church, which is the only church here with two bodies, the Board of Bishops form one, and the representatives of the clergy and laity in equal numbers the other. The policy of the Methodist Episcopal Church in providing that its bishops shall not take part in the legislation of the church was wise and conservative, and therefore precludes their being formed into one body. The separation, therefore, must be between the clerical and lay delegates; each forming one house, with some proper provision as to their presiding officers. Such a division is almost imperative in view of the numbers of the representatives of both orders. The number of delegates to which the General Conference would now be entitled would be four hundred and thirty (Discipline,

1884). With a proper change in the law of representation this should be composed of two hundred and fifteen members from each order, clerical and lay. This number is quite large enough for securing proper examination, sufficient discussion, and a wise conclusion as to any question. Neither body should be much larger, and they could not be less in number and give fair representation. It is submitted to the consideration of the church whether the same practical result would not be secured by the church in adopting the policy of two houses, that is gained by nations; and whether it would not do much to avoid the evident dangers that were so apparent in the last General Conference, and which are incident to all such bodies.

Another thought is worth consideration, viz.: that there is no necessity for the church meeting in General Conference every four years. Its laws are well settled, its Discipline requires but little change, its ritual is acceptable, the doctrines are fixed. The details of organization, the revision of the work of the church and of the bishops, the election of bishops, of the official secretaries, editors and publishers, form the main work of the Conference. These meetings of the General Conference are attended with heavy expense in money and in time. The entertainment of such a body involves a charge on the memberships that few places can meet.

There is danger in the frequent assembling of legislators of every kind, unless there are matters of importance that demand consideration. Such subjects come up in the earlier and formative state of governments and of the church; and when the wants and development of a country or of a church are rapid in their growth, they must be met by legislation; but neither of these reasons have much force at this time in the Methodist Episcopal Church. There are in all organizations either ambitious men who want to distinguish themselves, or religious nihilists who would destroy where they cannot rule, and who are ever ready to introduce questions which do no good and therefore are injurious.

The judgment of all prudent men in State management inclines to limit legislative sessions, either by a fixed number of days, by restricting pay, by making them biennial, or by combining both restrictions, as in the State of Pennsylvania. Would there not be safety in limiting the meeting of the General Conference to once in six years? It would at least help to prevent many of the evils which have appeared in former Conferences and that were so potent in the last, and would give more time to test the efficiency and wisdom of changes that have been made. Frequent changes in the laws of the state or church are always injurious.

DEFECTS OF THE GENERAL CONFERENCE AS A LEGISLATIVE BODY.

That some protective changes are required in the constitution of the General Conference was made evident in its last session. No one could carefully watch the proceedings in 1884 without noting that it was not in a high sense a deliberative body. The work in the committees may have been well and thoroughly done, but when their reports came up for consideration, the chief aim of the body seemed to be to allow the least possible time for their consideration, and the race was an equal one, between the presiding bishop and some member calling the previous question, as to which could the most quickly stop discussion. The proceedings seemed based on the idea that either the committee's report should be adopted, or that all the members were so well informed as to need no light, or were unwilling to receive any further information on the subject before them. The condensation of thought in many of the speeches only suggested the arguments and facts; no room was left to show their application. A secretary of the Missionary Society was stopped by time when giving information on a point before the Conference which he alone could give, and which was indispensable in the formation of a proper judgment.

Another evidence of the absence of proper care was seen in the reception of and action on recommendations of the Committee on Revisals. Those familiar with the course proposed changes in the Discipline take, understand how readily important changes in the law of the church may be made and adopted by the General Conference, without either the committee or the Conference understanding the intention or the effect of such changes. This possibility is inherent in the methods pursued, and is not due to wilful inattention to duty. To this cause are to be attributed many of the changes that have to be made by each General Conference to harmonize former action. The absence of any properly-arranged codification or intelligent digest of the laws of the church renders the necessity of greater care in making changes the more evident. The required approval of two separate bodies would do much to correct this evil. The use of "the previous question" to stop discussion is a necessary form in all large deliberative or legislative bodies. It is the only protection that such bodies have against obstructive tactics, whether of good or evil intent, but it is a dangerous power and should be cautiously used. The very fact of its constant use proves that there was a felt necessity to hurry through the business of the Conference in order that its session might not be unduly prolonged, the result being that the proper discussion of important questions was prevented to meet such lack of time, with its consequent unwise legislation. This haste was a serious defect in a body charged with the consideration and direction of such great interests. The General Conference is not singular in this respect. The same difficulty has been present in General Conventions of the Episcopal Church, and in General Assemblies of the Presbyterian Church. It is inherent in all large representative bodies. It is said that deliberation in legislation in the House of Commons (the largest representative body in the world) is only possible through the continued absence of a large proportion of its members. Obstruction and imperfect legislation are natural outgrowths of all large deliberative bodies.

Then, too, the action of the Conference was unreliable; for the body was frequently carried away by the spread-eagleism of a Methodism turning somebody loose on the world, and that the world was the parish of Methodist itinerants, etc. Questions, as well as elections, were carried by misplaced sympathy. There was evidently a great want of careful thought and examination of the fitness of the candidates for all the offices, from the highest to the lowest. Arguments were used in favor of some that were unworthy and improper, showing a defective comprehension of duty on the part of the delegates using such arguments. There was a want of that broad-minded thought that should have characterized a body so important to the church and to the cause of Christ.

In addition to the want of deliberation in the body, and its action through unbalanced enthusiasm and sympathy, there was the undoubted presence of bargaining in selection of some of the persons to fill the highest, as well as other official places. The charge was deliberately made on the floor of the Conference, indignantly denied, and yet proved to be true by the results.

The members of the church were gratified with the result of the election for bishops in the Cincinnati Conference of 1880, and it was hoped the disgraceful scenes of the Brooklyn Conference of 1872 would not be repeated in 1884; but when three men were chosen from the West and one from the East to be bishops, it was no haphazard arrangement, and when two of the four had failed of an election by former Conferences and had been accepted as standing candidates for the office, it was evidently no chance vote that elected them. The very unanimity with which a successor was chosen and elected to fill the place of a Book Agent in Cincinnati proved that bargaining and exchange of votes had been successful. How far the colored vote was manipulated to secure these results may yet be revealed. It is a misfortune for the men who were thus elected, whether they were parties to the agreements and combinations or not, because it places them under a cloud and affects their acceptability to the church. And for the purpose of this argument it is of little importance how far such agreements and bargainings were successful in these and other instances; the lesson to be learned from this and former experiences is, that no church can afford to have its highest places filled either by unworthy men or by the tactics of the politician. The peculiar position of a bishop in the Methodist Episcopal Church before the church and country, standing, as he does, between the ministry and the laity, demands the implicit confidence of the church to make his administration successful. The members must see to it that some plan be adopted which will do away with or lessen the dangers to which the General Conference is now exposed from the lack of deliberation, the momentary gush of sentimental sympathy in the wrong place, and combinations to secure the offices of the church. It is with a sad heart that such hard words are written, but the evils spoken of are so great and so apparent that it would be a wrong to omit a notice of them in an essay of this kind.

These evils would be lessened by the presence of an equal number of laymen in the Conference, and yet more by the institution of separate houses. The business education of the laity prepares their minds to fairly consider questions, to weigh evidence, to judge of character, ability, and adaptation of men to perform any given work. They are not easily led away by enthusiasm, sentimentality, or sympathy; and as they are not candidates for the episcopate, and as the general officers of the church are generally ministers, the laity will have little of personal interest to influence them, and can the better decide who should be chosen for any place. They are the better judges of the fitness of ministers to perform a given work.

THE SELECTION OF OFFICIALS.

Too great care cannot be taken to secure as bishops men who are the best suited for such a position by their physical condition, mental capacity, training, and acquirements; by their acceptability in the pulpit; by the possession of a judicial habit of mind; by clearness and quickness of apprehension; by knowledge of men and ability to read character; by tact in dealing with men under the trying circumstances that every Annual Conference produces; by warm sympathy, and by their acknowledged piety. A few errors in the choice of bishops would put a severe strain on the organization of the church; unless they command its respect and confidence, they will affect its administration, its harmony and prosperity. The successful working of the itinerancy and the unification of the church largely depend on their wisdom and prudence. It must be evident to all who are acquainted with the usual means taken to select candidates for this office, and who have a lively remembrance of the elections by the General Conferences of 1872 and 1884, that the church cannot risk her prosperity and usefulness by their continuation; that some plan must be adopted which will require a general unanimity of sentiment to secure an election. The experience of 1872 and 1884 certainly proves that a body constituted as those General Conferences were cannot make a wise selection of men for an office that carries with it such responsibilities, that requires such preparation and positive qualities, and that is so intimately connected with the prosperity of the church.

The Methodist Episcopal Church cannot afford to lower the standard of episcopal qualifications. There should even be more care taken in the selection of bishops than in the earlier days, because their duties are becoming more difficult to perform. The increasing numbers in both orders (clerical and lay), the increasing difficulty of securing a knowledge of the ministry, the wants of the people, the country, and the higher wants of the church, all tend to demand enlarged capacity of mind, judgment, prudence, and administrative ability in the occupants of the office. It is therefore important to improve, by change of law, upon the present uncertain way of selecting men for that position, and this independently of all questions of bargain or other improper influences. There must be provision made that will give time to carefully examine into the fitness or unfitness of the men nominated. The propositions to require the lay and clerical delegates to meet apart during an election (if they are not organized into two separate bodies), and to require a certain proportion of both—that is, more than a majority—to make an election, are therefore prudent, protective, and conservative. Other precautions may be taken; too much care cannot be exercised.

The question of the best method of selecting persons to fill the other offices in the church deserves further consideration. Three points are required to be well met:

First: The competency of the person.

Second: The establishment of a direct responsibility to the General Conference.

Third: The avoidance of danger to the church from intrigue, bargain, or electioneering for an office.

The present plan of electing secretaries, publishing-agents, and editors is defective in all these points. The election of officers by a mass-meeting of over four hundred delegates gives no security that the persons elected have any positive or peculiar fitness for their work. Such elections open the way to all the perils of intrigue and corruption.

There is now no proper responsibility. The managers of the boards defend themselves for any mishap or defect by the fact that the secretaries are not of their choosing, the members of the General Conference that they are not the executive body, and the secretaries that either they had not proper support or they assumed that all they did was proper and all criticism unjust. The secretaries and agents, as now elected, are, in fact, the only responsible parties; the managers are but advisers. This accounts for the tone of superiority assumed by some secretaries and agents over the boards.

It has been suggested that the secretaries and agents could be better selected, and much of the danger from intrigue in the General Conference be avoided, by the appointment of a committee of its body to nominate to the Conference not less than two and not more than three persons for each office, from which the Conference may select. This would be a step in advance of the present method, but it fails in establishing proper responsibility. In all well-managed bodies the executive officers are appointed by the representatives of the owners or of parties interested; this secures a direct line of responsibility. The executive officers are responsible to the managers or directors, and they in their turn are responsible to the proprietors or parties in interest. Such a common-sense principle should be adopted by the General Conference. It can be done, First: By the careful selection of the managers of the different boards and the Book Room Committee; and, Second: By giving them the power to elect the secretaries, Book Room agents, and editors; such selection being governed by the rule that effective travelling ministers should be selected when the duties of the office required ministerial education and the use of ministerial functions, and laymen when such duties were of a business nature.

This plan would secure secretaries, agents, and editors better fitted for their places and with more assurance of success; it would place responsibility in the right place, and have a strong tendency to prevent the dangers described from strife for office. It would also be an inducement to men to give up their time wholly to their official duties, knowing that their services would be continued if they were faithful to their work, and that they would not be liable to be dropped at the end of every four years. It would also enable the managers to make changes in officers in case of their deficiency or inability to fill a place. A more intelligent and efficient working of all the church interests would be the result, and the church would be saved from scandal and from the dangers that threaten its usefulness at this point.

There was an evident disposition in the last General Conference to attack the bishops, to overrule their recommendations, and to lower their influence in the body for the purpose of producing certain changes in their relation to the church. These efforts will be more fully described hereinafter. The church has not much to be proud of in the proceedings of the last General Conference; the members may congratulate themselves, however, that much greater evils were prevented by the presence of the lay representatives; as in all other religious bodies, their conservatism was the saving influence.

The changes in the construction of the General Conference that this discussion has developed, as required for the well-being of the Methodist Episcopal Church, are:

First: Equal representation, clerical and lay.

Second: Such representation to be based wholly on the number of members, without regard to the number of the ministers in an Annual Conference.

Third: The readjustment of the relation of the mission, foreign, and colored Conferences to the General Conference.

Fourth: That only the effective travelling ministers shall be eligible as clerical representatives in General Conference, including educators, and excluding the superannuated, the supernumerary ministers, the secretaries of the different boards, the editors, and Book Agents.

Fifth: That the choice of bishops shall be made from ministers who are not members of the General Conference, and that no member of a General Conference shall be eligible to any official place in the church.

Sixth: That the members of the General Conference shall be divided into two bodies, the one composed of the lay delegates, and the other of the clerical delegates, each body to be presided over as may be determined; that all action by the Conference shall require the assent of a majority of both bodies, and that in elections to the office of bishop care shall be taken to secure, by the requirement of some certain proportion of each body, the nearest practicable approach to unanimity of sentiment. As to committees and persons elected to offices, a majority vote of both orders should be required.

Until these changes are made all elections should require a majority of both orders, clerical and lay, the vote being taken by orders, meeting separately and apart from each other.

Seventh: That the General Conference shall meet but once in six years.

Eighth: That the secretaries of the Conference boards, the agents of the Book Concern, and all editors, shall be elected by the respective Board of Managers and by the Book Committee.

II. The Annual Conference.

The next body in rank of importance in the Methodist Episcopal Church is the Annual Conference. Its construction and relation to the General Conference have been stated. The establishment of this body was another of those wise provisions for which the form of government of the Methodist Episcopal Church is so noted, and was admirably suited to the work of the earlier church, and equally consistent in its provisions with the views of the Fathers, that the church of God should be governed by the ministers.

The Annual Conference meets yearly at some point in the district or country assigned to it by the next preceding General Conference. It is presided over by one of the bishops, whose decisions are subject to the right of an appeal to the next General Conference for its final decision. Its members are the ministers of the church within its borders. They are called travelling preachers in contradistinction to the local preachers. They are called effective preachers when they are able to accept appointments and perform the work required. When non-effective they are placed in the superannuated or supernumerary ranks, as the case may be. The ministers belong to the church at large; they are attached to Conferences for the convenience of administration, and may be transferred from any one Confererce or district of country to another. Every effective minister is entitled, at the hands of the bishop presiding, to an appointment to some charge every year, but to no charge for more than three successive years. The work done by him, his character and usefulness, are passed under review at every Annual Conference. The condition of the station or circuit to which he was attached is stated in open Conference, with the amount of contributions to the official societies and boards of the church. To render this very thorough examination possible, and to provide for the careful supervision of the ministry and the different charges, and also to understand and meet, as far as possible, the religious wants of the country embraced within the bounds of the Conference, such Conference districts are divided up into two or more subdistricts, over which a minister, selected for his wisdom, experience, and godly character, is appointed by the presiding bishop every year, and may be reappointed for four successive years. He is called a presiding elder. It is the duty of the presiding elders, at each meeting of the Annual Conference, to give the bishop the benefit of their observation and judgment upon the condition and wants of each station and circuit, the general religious condition and wants of the country embraced within their districts, and the appointments to be made. The bishop having the exclusive power of appointment, the position of the presiding elder is simply advisory.

Such is the essence of the itinerancy, with its nicely-balanced system of adaptation and protection to the ministers and the church. Other points connected with it will be hereafter considered.

The Annual Conferences, composed as has been

stated, have the further duty of the examination and reception of applicants for the ministry, and have the power to elect them to deacon's and elder's orders, to try them for breaches of the Discipline, whether in morals or in the execution of their duties; to expel them, with a reserved right of appeal to the next General Conference; to locate and to grant them supernumerary or superannuated relations; and also to restore them to the full work of the ministry, except in cases of expulsion. The Annual Conferences generally take cognizance of all societies connected with the interests of the church within its borders, such as missionary, Bible, tract, and benevolent societies, and they distribute the moneys raised for the support of the worn-out ministers, their widows and orphans.

The above detail has been given that the further consideration of the organization and functions of such Conferences might be more clearly understood. It will have been noted that the assured life of any Annual Conference lasts but four years, the General Conference establishing its metes and bounds at every quadrennial session; that it has no autonomy in and of itself. Its boundaries may be enlarged, divided up into one, two, or more Conferences; it may disappear, being sliced up like Poland, and its territory given to other Conferences; its name may be changed or blotted out. It exists merely as a wise provision for performing certain executive work of the church, such as "the admission of preachers on trial and into full connection, the ordination of elders and deacons, the examination of the characters of the ministers and preachers, and the stationing of them all, as well as the management of the fund for the superannuated preachers,"* its members having no rights arising from their connection with any specific Conference. What rights they may have are as provided for in the Discipline. They are members of the Methodist Episcopal Church as the laity are; they are ministers in the Methodist Episcopal Church at large; have an equal power in the control of the sheep of the pasture, and are on an equality with their brethren; they all have the right to a yearly appointment to some station, circuit, mission, and to such support as may be voluntarily given them by the people. The relation of the Annual Conferences to the General Conference, and of the rights of the ministers thereto, are important facts that deserve consideration.

The Annual Conference has no power of originating questions touching the polity of the church or its administration. It has no power of legislation and cannot have. Its powers are strictly defined and grow out of its special work. No superior body can give power to an inferior body to legislate upon any points that are material to the interests of the superior body without at least the power of revisal before ultimate action is taken. This, in the case of an Annual Conference, is impracticable, as it can, at most, last but four years, its existence legally ending at the next General Conference, which would revise its legislation. Unless all power of primary legislation were given to the An-

---

* Coke and Asbury on Discipline, 1796.

nual Conferences (they being constituted as a representative body for the purpose), and it were made the duty of the General Conference to pass on such legislation, there can properly be no legislative powers connected with Annual Conferences. Such power would involve a radical reorganization of the polity of the church, for which there is no necessity. What the future wants of the church may require, when it has increased to three, four, or five times its present membership, is a question that will be decided when the time comes.

It follows, then, from the nature of the Annual Conferences and the object of their formation, that they have no right to representation in the General Conference as such; the right is in the ministry as individuals.

WHO SHOULD BE MEMBERS OF AN ANNUAL CONFERENCE.

The original idea of membership of, or connection with, an Annual Conference was, that the preachers who were in the active work within the limits of each Conference should meet together once a year, in order that the bishop might meet with them and assign them to their work. Time soon developed the necessity of creating superannuated and supernumerary relations, which was done, with a continuation of all rights and powers as ministers of the church. These relations continue to the present time. In considering who should be attached to an Annual Conference, a proper test would be the character of the work done by the individual preacher within the bounds of a Conference.

The church may choose to continue in its clerical ranks all those who have been received and are in good standing without regard to their employment, but may refuse to give all of them the right of membership in an Annual Conference, or may select to whom it will give such right. These positions are and should be recognized as distinct. Preachers may be refused the last relation, while they are given or continued in the former. With this distinction the terms of membership in an Annual Conference may be more readily fixed. The propriety of including as members in an Annual Conference the preachers who receive their regular yearly appointments to stations, circuits, and missions passes without query, for the Conference was instituted for their convenience and for this purpose. There are after these, three classes of work to which preachers in full connection with the Conferences have been yearly assigned, and which do not come under the rules of the itinerancy: First, Presidents and professors in theological schools, universities, colleges, and other schools of learning in connection with the church; Secondly, Agents of Bible and other benevolent societies which are not under the control of the church; and, Thirdly, Preachers who have been selected by the General Conference as secretaries of its benevolent boards.

What relation should such preachers hold to the Conference? The evident test is, as stated, the character of their work. The same reasons which would make it proper that professors in our theological schools and educators in our different institutions of learning should be eligible as delegates to the General Conference would make them members of an Annual Conference. The converse of this rule would not apply to the secretaries of the boards and official editors of the press of the church, who, while excluded from membership of the General Conference for prudential reasons which have been fully discussed, yet should retain their connection with an Annual Conference. The Secretary of the American Bible Society or of any State Bible organization, when a Methodist preacher, should retain his relation to an Annual Conference; this work is so important, so fundamental to the cause of the Christian religion, that its chief agents are entitled to special recognition. The Book Agents, and the secretaries and agents associated with societies outside the control of the General Conference have no just claim to membership in a Conference, because such membership is not required for the performance of their duties. Then comes the class of ministers bearing the relation of superannuates and supernumeraries. What possible claim can they have to membership, *per se*, in a Conference? They may be made amenable to a Conference for the examination of their characters without being members thereof. These brethren who would be thus deprived of membership may still, as suggested, hold their clerical relation to the church at large, their exclusion from an Annual Conference being based on the fact that they have no proper relation as ministers to its business. Other and personal reasons will be hereafter given for such exclusion; the one just stated is broad enough to justify such action. An objection to this suggestion will be made: that it deprives such men of all representation in the church councils. It does as ministers, but are these brethren any more worthy than the bishops of the church, who have no right of representation? But they have the advantage of the bishops in that they can accept their proper relation to the church as local preachers, when for any reason they fail to perform their full duty as efficient travelling preachers. By this change they may be elevated to an equality with their brethren and sisters,—the laity,—and thereby secure representation. If the church would clearly understand the proper work of an Annual Conference, the distinction between the relation of the preachers to it and their relation to the church, there would be little difficulty in arriving at a solution of some of the troublesome questions connected with those holding supernumerary and superannuated relations. A return to the original conception of an Annual Conference, with the recognition of the proper work of the ministers in it, would be a great deliverance from many evils that have for years been developing into importance.

LAY REPRESENTATIVES IN ANNUAL CONFERENCES.

The propriety and policy of the membership in Annual Conferences being confined exclusively to the preachers has been frequently discussed. The General Conference of 1876 appointed a committee to report on a plan for introducing lay representation into such Conferences. The General Conferences of 1880 and 1884, though plans were laid before them by the proper committee, yet refused to take any action to adopt the same. Such refusal came, not from a want of understanding the merits of the question nor from the lack of time, but from an opposition to the proposed measure.

Such continued refusal to admit lay representatives into the Annual Conferences demands a careful investigation of the arguments and reasons adduced on both sides of the question.

It is acknowledged that such introduction would be a radical change in the theory and policy of the church as to the Annual Conferences; that it is not essential to the mere administrative work of the Conference, that it can only be demanded on the principle of the recognition of the "priesthood of believers," and on the broad grounds of increased security to the polity of the church, added care in the acceptance of candidates for the ministry, for the protection of the character of the ministers, of better provision for their support, of meeting the widening work of the church in its various fields of benevolence, and the constantly enlarging local interests of each Conference district.

There has been a great increase in the number of interests that are brought under the care of the Annual Conferences. They open to the church new and varied fields of labor, and are a natural product of its religious teachings. The care of these interests was not anticipated as part of the work of an Annual Conference. Yet as the Conference is the immediate representative body of the church in its district, these properly come under its oversight and are entitled to its protection.

The decision of this question of the introduction of lay representatives in the Annual Conference thus depends on the influence such representation would have on all the interests just named. The course of an examination of the proposed change is thus fairly marked out.

The fundamental argument is in the rights of "the believers." These rights have been defined in the principles already established of the proper constitution of the General Conference, or of the government of any associated body of Christians. They are inherent in the natural and scriptural right and duty of the members of Christ's body, to manage the interests of His church as a whole, or as a matter of greater convenience by representation from the whole body. These rights are superior to any polity, laws, customs, or habits of the church, and when necessity or prudence demand their exercise, such polity, laws, customs, or habits must yield. If these principles were accepted, the Annual Conference would be composed of representatives from all the stations and circuits, without regard to whether their duty might be to teach or to support the teachers. If this end were secured, all the work of the Conferences could be accomplished. But here, as in the case of the General Conference, comes in the force of old habits, established customs, usages, etc.; and while the best form of organization cannot be had, the next best may in time be secured, viz.: the equal representation in numbers of the laity and the ministry, with equal power in every respect. This would be after the example of the Presbytery in the Presbyterian Churches, of the Convention in the Episcopal Churches, and of the Classis in the German Churches.

If this ratio of representation cannot be secured, it may be more prudent to secure the recognition of the principle, that at first some fixed number shall be selected by each district in the Conference, as was suggested by the report on this subject made to the General Conference of 1880. If this were done, such lay representatives should have the same rights and powers that are now given to the lay representatives in the General Conference. The objections to this reduced ratio of representation may have to be borne with for a time, until the increased intelligence and broadened views of the church, with the acknowledged good results of the presence of lay members, shall secure a change to the better basis of equality in numbers and direct representation.

What objections can be made to this or the former plan? Would they lessen the efficiency of the church? Would any inherited rights be invaded? Would they lessen the efficiency of the Annual Conferences? Would either of them in any way interfere with carrying on the proper business of an Annual Conference? Would not such introduction of laymen naturally aid in the transaction of its business and promote its usefulness?

The objections made to the admittance of laymen into the Annual Conferences, with full and equal powers, have generally been,—

First: That it would make the Conferences too large, and that they could not, as now, be accommodated in the cities, towns, and villages where their annual sessions may be held.

Secondly: That the principal work of such a Conference having reference to the admission, examination, and ordination of the ministry, passing of character, and the reception of their appointments, there is but little for the laity to do.

Thirdly: That in many Conferences the laity serve on committees which consider and report upon many of the subjects that come up before the Conference.

Fourthly: That ministers should not be tried by laymen in an Annual Conference unless laymen are as liable to be tried by the ministry.

Let us consider these objections. If the principle is correct that the laity, as of "the priesthood of believers," should be admitted into the councils of the church: if the cause of Christ, the only object of the existence of a church, would be thereby promoted, then all objections as to numbers fail. But arrangements can be made to meet every need of the church. For instance, the adoption of the recommendation as to terms of membership in an Annual Conference would materially reduce its numbers. The people would be relieved from the accepted duty of entertaining the long line of attached ministers in the form of superannuates, supernumeraries, etc. What occasion is there for the presence of the young men who are applicants for admission or examination? They could be represented as well absent as present; the personal examination of their faces and persons amounts to nothing, for the most unpromising-looking subjects have been admitted. The General Conference has not established any standard of physical beauty or size as the criterion to judge by; if there were anything in this, it might more safely be left to a jury of the mothers in the church. The applicants for admission and the preachers on trial could be examined before the meeting of the Conference. The candidates for orders need only to be present on the day of ordination. The number of the members advances with the population of the cities, towns, and villages, and the increased numbers of an Annual Conference would thus find increased accommodation. The objection as to numbers will not bear examination.

The second objection is based on the idea that the ministers are a separate order of human beings; that by being called to preach the gospel of Jesus Christ they are thereby exalted above their brethren; that they have by this call become the lords of Zion, and can only be criticised, examined, or tried by their peers, as they vainly term them. It is time such nonsense were driven out of the minds of Methodist ministers; it is mortifying to the laity that such thoughts exist among men whom they delight to reverence, honor, love, and uphold. What is there in the call to preach that should separate them from their brethren? What does the call involve? All that is included in it, by the teaching of the Scriptures as exemplified by Jesus Christ while on earth, is that the Holy Spirit may show to some persons that it is their duty to give up the ordinary occupations of life and devote themselves to preaching and teaching the gospel of the Son of God. As to other persons no communication is made, nor is needed, because the faithful performance of their duty to themselves, their families, their country, and their God comes to them with their growth. This is their natural duty; to give up the ordinary occupations of life and devote one's time to preaching Christ is a special duty. The laity are as fully performing their work in attending to the affairs of life as the ministers are in preaching the gospel. It is acknowledged with great pleasure that a call to preach is the highest honor that can be conferred on man; but it imposes a duty,—it does not create any right or make any difference in the preacher's relation to his fellow-man.

Every member of Christ's Church is the peer of every other member as to his rights and relation to the church, though there may be differences in every other respect. There is, therefore, no ground for the claim that the ministry should be under the jurisdiction of the ministers only. The laymen who would be sent to the Annual Conferences would be the equals of the ministers in intelligence, piety, and devotion to the church. Not one word will be written here that would in any wise tend to undervalue the character or the services of the ministers, nor will they be permitted to undervalue the laity by basing their rejection from the councils of the church on their ignorance, incapacity, lack of piety, or devotion to its interests. It is for the ministry to accept one or the other horns of the question. If they have faith in the laity of the church, and have gotten rid of priestly notions of superiority, then they will favor the introduction of lay representation into all the councils of the church. If they persist in refusing such introduction, the laity will be forced to the conclusion that every such minister is governed either by the notion of his superiority in the Church of God, or is not willing to trust the laity.

The experience of other churches where the laymen unite with the ministers on terms of perfect equality, and help to determine all questions relating to admission or ministerial relations, is an evidence in favor of such power being secured to the laity of the Methodist Episcopal Church in the Annual and General Conferences. The Methodist ministry are certainly of no higher grade than the ministry of other Christian churches. If there would be any difference in relative fitness, it would be in favor of making the laity the exclusive judges of ministerial character, for they are more deeply interested in the character, attainments, piety, and usefulness of the ministry. Then, too, they do not judge so harshly, they have no petty jealousies, no snubbings or slights to remember; they are not in the way of the growth, rise, or increasing influence of any one; nor do they uncharitably criticise their brethren's addresses, sermons, or other efforts. They are free from many evils that affect the relations of ministers to each other; their judgment would be based on facts, and less on sympathy or unkind feeling; they know the young men who have gone out from among them, and follow them with a fatherly or motherly interest.

The objection, then, to the laity exercising equal power in the Annual Conference so far as it may affect the ministry is unsound. True, it puts them on a par, for Conference purposes, with the laity; this may not be pleasant, but it is Christ's plan. The presence of lay members in an Annual Conference would do much towards checking the disposition of the ministry to arrogate to themselves power as a class, as a party, as a caste.

There is much proper work for the laity to do in the Annual Conference, in carefully guarding the entrance to the ministry, in watching the development of the young men in pulpit ability, in their acceptability as pastors, and in piety; in protecting the ministry and the church from men who have become unfitted for their high calling; in sympathizing with and encouraging those who may have made a misstep, through temptation, that they may be restored to their work. From such nearer relations to the ministry they could better understand their wants, sympathize with them in their trials, and rejoice with them in their successes. In very many ways the presence of the laity in the Annual Conferences would be a blessing to the church.

The third objection, that the laity are now members of committees in some of the Annual Conferences, and that nothing would be gained by their presence as members, is a quibble, because it is evident to every one, and to no one more clearly than to the ministers, that it is quite a different position to be on a committee without power even to advocate or to vote for its recommendations in the chief body, and to be a member of such a body with the right to originate and discuss questions; to have a potential voice and the full right of voting. The fact of the admission of laymen on committees in the Annual Conference is an acknowledgment of the strength of the argument in favor of their admission to the Conference as members.

As the Conferences have immediate charge and oversight of the benevolent societies, and of the educational institutions of the church within their limits, the importance of proper care of these interests cannot be overestimated. To bring these interests home to the members, the laity must assist in all action of the Conference referring thereto. There seems to be much difficulty in impressing on the minds of the ministers the fact that the laity have far more influence with each other than they (the ministers) have. Much of the ministers' work in such lines is perfunctorily done, as a matter of business, in the ways of their duty. When a layman takes an interest in such work, it is more as a matter of conviction.

A fourth objection was made on the floor of the General Conference, and it may be well to expose it, as its seeming justice may influence some one. The objection was, that it would be very unseemly for laymen to try ministers, since ministers cannot try laymen. Here again is the essence of ministerial aristocracy,— the argument of "Touch me not, for I am holier than thou." The objection has two parts,—first, that there is no inherent right in the church (that is, "the body of believers") to try a minister, and, second, that if it is done there should be a *quid pro quo*.

The doctrine of the relation of the ministry to the body of the church has been frequently stated in these pages; the ministry are not a separate body, but are of the "body of believers." This "body of believers" (the church) has all the power in itself to regulate its members, and has the same power through its representatives. This "body" can adopt different ways of trying ministers, both preachers on trial, deacons and elders, and of trying members in full connection and on probation. To whomsoever the duty of trying is delegated, they stand in the position of the church, of the whole "body of believers." This is the principle adopted by all evangelical churches. The objection, then, is in harmony with the assumption of priestly exclusiveness, of priestly superiority, and of priestly power over the laity; it is the argument of absolutists in church government.

The *quid pro quo* argument is puerile, for, as a matter of fact, the ministry have the laity under constant oversight, as provided for in the laws of the church, and that the church ("the body of believers") should provide that the ministry should be tried by a mixed jury of ministers and laymen is just as reasonable and consistent.

But finally. The principle of the union of ministers and laymen in trying a preacher is already part of the law of the church, for by the constitution of the General Conference, the bishops are judged by the ministry and laity jointly. If, then, the highest ministers in the church are under this joint jurisdiction, what argument is left why other ministers should be exempted from such jurisdiction? Though a bishop may be tried for immorality by a court of ministers, his appeal goes to the General Conference for its ultimate determination.

A further reason why the laity should be represented in the Annual Conferences will be found in the fact that, while they have to bear the burden of the support of the ministry, they should have a voice in determining the extent of that burden, and for whom it should be undertaken. As the law now stands, they are without power or influence at either of these points; the ministry may increase their numbers to any extent, and of any material; the bishops must give appointments to those whom the Conferences elect; circuits must be divided up into weak churches to make places for them, and the laity must furnish them subsistence. As the law now stands, the laity as a body must accept as their Christian teachers any and every man the ministers choose to receive into the Conference; they have no power to prevent it. Is it any wonder, with this statement, that the bishops have so much difficulty in finding places for many of the ministers, and that there is so much of complaint as to support? The present power of the ministers in the Annual Conferences, in this respect, is too great; the church requires lay representation in the Annual Conference to protect both ministers and the laity here. There has been, and there is now, too little care taken by the ministers in receiving men into the Conferences; there is, too, a great difference between bearing a burden and placing it on others. Every member knows how readily young men are persuaded by over-anxious mothers and friends to enter the ministry. The highest ambition of an Irish family is to have one of its sons in the priesthood. There is much of this feeling in Methodism. Every member also knows the influences that are brought to bear on Quarterly Conferences to recommend young men to the Annual Conferences, and how few of the ministers can face the loss of the kind entertainment, or personal attachment, by a vote against the acceptance of a son, or a brother, or of a friend of the family. Every member also knows that there is but little difficulty in squeezing the candidates through an Annual Conference Committee, receiving them on trial and in time electing them to deacon's orders, though they may have to agree to be transferred to another Conference. In an earlier day, when there was a great demand for preachers, the Conferences might have been justified in admitting into their close corporation young and married men who were not properly prepared, and who did not give promise of any special adaptation to the work. The case is different now. Each applicant should be closely examined, and only those admitted who after proper trial can reasonably be expected to show themselves workmen worthy of their high calling.

There is a point yet to be thought over, which in its full weight is probably of more importance to the safety of the church than any yet named. It is found in the fact that by the present law a change in any of the "Restrictive Rules," except the one relating to "Articles of Religion," can be made by the "concurrent recommendation of three-fourths of all the members of the several Annual Conferences, who shall be present and vote on such recommendation, followed by a majority of two-thirds of the General Conference succeeding." It will be noticed that this law gives to the ministry absolute power over all the polity of the church; they may strip the church of everything that is special and peculiar to it,—its itinerancy, its class-meetings, its love-feasts, its Sunday-schools, its missionary and other boards; the whole framework of the church may be removed; the only thing they cannot destroy is its "Articles of Religion."*

The object of submitting proposed changes in the "Restrictive Rules" to the Annual Conferences was evidently to use them as a ready way of getting an expression of opinion from the ministry. It might have been done otherwise, but the annual meetings of the Conferences afforded the benefit of discussion and an easier way of securing a vote. This is also evident from the law requiring the assent of a three-fourth majority of the members of all the Conferences, for by this condition, and in this way, a majority of three-fourths of the ministry is secured.† No argument in favor of the autonomy of the Annual Conference can be drawn from the submission to them of so important a matter as a change of the law of the church.

These provisions, requiring the majorities as stated, are in the line of conservatism so far as the ministers are interested; but while they are conservative as to the ministry, there is in them not one particle of protection for the church itself,—that is, for the members. The presence of the lay representatives in the General Con-

---

* It is admitted that the lay vote in the General Conference is a check on the ministerial power. But unless taken as a separate vote, how slight the check is!

† The initiation of a change in the "Restrictive Rules" can be made by the ministers in the Annual Conferences, but not by the Annual Conferences as such. This distinction should be kept in mind.

ference as now organized affords but little protection, because they have no separate vote on changes in the "Restrictive Rules," but are merged into the whole body. It is but the plainest right that the laity should have a voice in the determination of the fundamental laws of the church. Why should the power to change and alter everything in Methodism, except its "Articles of Religion," be limited to the ministry? Why should a membership of nearly two millions be excluded from every and all legalized expression of their opinions on proposed changes in the fundamental laws of the church?

The object of requiring such majorities of the Annual Conferences was conservative, and designed to secure a full vote of the ministry. Why should not a vote of the laity be included, and thereby evidence be given that the Methodist Episcopal Church is not a church of the ministry only, but of the people, as Christ intended? Is not all good reason in favor of submitting any and all changes in the constitution of a church to the members thereof, either directly or indirectly, through their representatives? Are not changes in the constitutions of the States so submitted? Is the membership of the Methodist Episcopal Church less fitted to judge of the merits of changes in its laws than the people at large of a State to judge of important changes in State constitutions? There can be but one kind of answers to these questions. How, then, can such expression of the laity be the most easily obtained? Extend the practice of the church in getting an expression from the ministry so as to include the laity, then the presence of the laymen in equal numbers in the Annual Conferences will afford a direct method of securing such an expression; and further, a vote of three-fourths of the ministers present and of three-fourths of the lay representatives would probably express the opinion of the whole membership, including the ministry, as well as it can be obtained.

With the laity properly represented in the Annual Conferences, the duties of such bodies would be performed with greater safety to the rights of the ministry and membership and with increased efficiency. With equal representation in both the Annual and General Conferences, the general polity of the Methodist Episcopal Church would be reasonably assured by the presence of the conservatism needed in all deliberative bodies. The propriety of the introduction of the laity into the Annual Conferences as a matter of their right and interest in the "Restrictive Rules" of the church cannot be questioned.

An argument may be fairly drawn from the positive advantages connected with such introduction of the laity into the Annual Conferences. These can be generally stated. Certain dangers to be hereafter noted would be lessened, the church would be unified in its interests, its resources would be strengthened, its efforts would be enlarged, its piety would be increased, the ministry would be more trusted, respected, reverenced, and be better cared for. The ministers who oppose lay representation in the Annual Conferences make a great mistake; they stand in the way of their personal interests and in that of the progress of Christ's cause.

The proposed changes in the construction of the Annual Conference will then comprise:

First: That until the conditions of membership of the Annual Conferences shall be changed, the right to vote shall be limited to the effective travelling preachers, including presiding elders, station and circuit and mission preachers, secretaries of the official benevolent boards, ministers engaged as educators in colleges, universities, or schools under the patronage of one or more Annual Conferences, secretaries of the American Bible Society or of any State Bible Society, editors of the church papers, and professors and teachers in theological schools.

Second: That lay representatives shall be admitted in such numbers as may be determined from each district, who shall in all respects be the equals of the ministry in the sessions of the Conference; this to include the right to a vote on all questions affecting the ministry, including their admission, their advancement, trial, location, or the granting any other relation, and on changes in the "Restrictive Rules," and to a separate vote on the same basis as provided for in the General Conference.

INCORPORATION OF ANNUAL CONFERENCES.

In the line of legal provisions in the Discipline, by which the character of the Annual Conferences and their relation to the General Conference and the church have been changed, and whereby the balance of the organization between the clergy and the laity must be disturbed, if not altogether broken, is to be found a very significant and remarkable addition to the powers and duties of the Annual Conferences, as made by the General Conference of 1876. This provision heads the list in the legislation as to the Annual Conference, as follows (Discipline, 1884):

"There are now one hundred and three Annual Conferences in the year, and these shall severally become bodies corporate, wherever practicable, under the authority of the law of the States and Territories within whose boundary they are located."

While it may be something to be grateful for, that there are now one hundred and three Annual Conferences in the church, yet this is evidently but a prefix to cover the more important fact that, by the latter part of the paragraph, it is made the duty of such Conferences to seek for corporate powers from the proper State and Territorial authorities. This act of the General Conference involves so much of danger to the church that it demands most careful consideration and exposure.

The first question that is suggested is, Should Annual Conferences be intrusted with corporate rights? It can scarcely be argued that an inferior and subordinate body should be clothed with powers that the superior body, its creator, has not given and could not give. The General Conference is not an incorporated body, nor is there any necessity that it should be for the performance of its duties. It has no property, it inherits no money, it carries on no business; its expenses can be and are met by other means.

The Annual Conference is, as has been described, a

mere convenience of the church to carry out its work. It is wholly in the power of the General Conference; all the Annual Conferences may be removed from the polity of the church and cease to have an existence. Now wherein is there any reason why such bodies should be clothed with corporate powers, by which they are placed beyond the control of the General Conference, powers too which are not required in the performance of their administrative duties? The next questions are, Can Annual Conferences receive corporate powers? Are they fit subjects for such powers? The description already given of the authority by which they exist, and of the objects for which they exist, entirely precludes the idea of there being any fitness in bestowing such powers upon them. Corporate rights are only given to bodies that are to be permanent, that are controlled by the parties interested in them, or by managers duly selected. In every one of these conditions of fitness for corporate powers an Annual Conference fails. The requisite conditions arise from the relation to and contract with the State which grants the power. Corporate bodies are to be useful and of advantage to the public weal; they are to be subject to the control of the State, its taxing authority, and the processes of law. There must be responsibility connected with all corporations; some person with whom the courts can deal. The Annual Conference has no stability; it is under the control of a body beyond the power of any State court; its membership may be entirely changed at the end of any year, and its own existence at the end of every four years; there is no responsibility connected with it. No State Legislature would grant any corporate authority to such a body if it understood its construction and relation to the church.

It may be argued that charters are given to church societies, and that the principle is the same. In answer to this it may be said that one object in using societies for church work is to meet the demands of the State by having a responsible party to whom to give the powers asked for, and who shall be answerable to the State's laws and its taxing authority. This is one defective point, hereinafter stated, as to the legal position of the church boards.

The next question to be asked is, What is to be the character of the powers asked for in a charter? The law in the Discipline was either very ignorantly drawn or drawn with the intention of having hid away in it what politicians call a snake. The church law requires simply that the Conferences shall become bodies corporate, leaving to each Conference to determine the character of the work it is to do, and for which corporate powers are to be secured. For all the General Conference can do after this general instruction, an Annual Conference may ask for corporate powers to run a distillery, to keep a gin palace, to build a railway, to run iron, cotton, or woollen factories, to publish newspapers filled with infidel teachings, to publish books in opposition to the Methodist Episcopal Church. There is no limit and no allusion to the objects of such charters. It is therefore not strange that no action has been taken on this law, and that it has remained a dead letter.

11*

If the object of the framers of the law was to enable the Annual Conferences to hold property or to secure bequests, which is a supposable case, then the objections that have been made to such power in a Conference on the ground of irresponsibility and uncertain life have full force, and there is the further objection that this method of holding property and receiving bequests for church and benevolent purposes is not necessary. All such bequests and property can be safely held for the benefit of the church through chartered societies or through trustees, avoiding doubtful questions of legality. That this is the judgment of good and able men is evinced by the fact that no church as an organic body has been chartered, and that they all work through societies and boards.

Having thus shown that an Annual Conference, by its formation and condition of life, is not fitted for the use of corporate powers, and that such powers are not required for the reception of bequests or the holding of property, they being better taken care of by societies, the next question will be, What would be the effect on the church if the Annual Conferences were to act on such instructions and receive corporate powers to be used in good directions?

In the first place, unless all the Conferences were limited by State or Territorial boundaries, there would be an inequality among them which would be unjust. Some would have powers which others could not possess. If they comprised parts of two or more States, then the State chartering could not control their action in another State.

Secondly: Unless the General Conference specified by statute the powers to be granted by such charters and how they should be used, there would be no two charters alike; ending in inevitable confusion, legal difficulties, expense, and disgrace.

Thirdly: Such chartered Conferences would upset the whole polity of Methodism. The possession of a charter would, first, prevent any change of Conference limits, either by adding to or taking from them. It would place personal responsibility on the members of one Conference that might be greater than in another, and it might secure more financial help to members of one Conference than to another. Such possibilities, and many of the same character, would destroy the policy of an itinerancy and of transfers. Any interference with the free movement of the organization of the church would be injurious. It would also affect the appointing power in many ways.

Fourthly: It would be building up financial interests in the church, wholly and absolutely in the power and under the control of the ministry. It would be laying the foundations of a spiritual hierarchy that would be destructive of the evangelical character and spiritual life of the church. It would add to the offices to be filled by the ministry; the temptation to the secularization of the ministry would be increased; the church would incur greater risk of injury and disgrace by the failure of the ministers to properly manage bequests, or to handle real and personal property.

There is danger to the church in having such a law in the Discipline,—it is marvellous that it has been permitted so many years of unmolested existence. Laws supposed to be dead and inoperative sometimes and very unexpectedly spring into life and cause trouble. Whatever may have been the object of the introduction of this one, it is time it should be erased from our statute book, or it may give trouble when least looked for. The laity in all the States should bear this possibility in mind and be prepared to defeat any attempt to secure corporate power for the Annual Conferences, either directly from legislatures or through general laws of incorporation.

The presence of such a law in the statute book of the church affords an additional argument in favor of securing a more careful examination of proposed changes of, or additions to, the Discipline than is possible in the General Conference as at present organized, and it points directly at the necessity of a full lay representation in the councils of the church, and further, the division of the General Conference into two bodies (clerical and lay).

III. The Quarterly Conference.

The third organized body in the church, the wheel within two wheels, is the Quarterly Conference.

It is composed of the stationed preacher, the attached superannuated and supernumerary preachers, the local preachers and exhorters connected with the station or circuit, the stewards, class-leaders, trustees of the church, and the superintendent of the Sunday-schools. The trustees and the superintendent must be members of the church and approved by the Quarterly Conference. The preacher in charge appoints the class-leaders and exhorters, and nominates the stewards and trustees (when not otherwise provided by State laws) to the Conference for their approval. The Conference gives license to local preachers and exhorters, and recommends candidates for the travelling ministry; it takes care of the spiritual and temporal interests of the church in each station or circuit; it performs an important part in the organization of the church, and is presided over by the elder of the district.

Its peculiar constitution was a natural outgrowth of the church in two directions.

First: That the power of control over the *personnel* of the Quarterly Conference might be retained by the preacher in charge, through the presence of the attached preachers, of the local preachers and the exhorters, and through his power of appointment and nomination. The result of this is, that the Quarterly Conference is a creature of the preacher in charge, controlled by men in sympathy with him, and by those who owe their membership either to his appointment or to his nomination. The right to nominate the stewards has always been considered a valuable prerogative of the ministry, as the stewards have charge of the ministers' support, and furnish a medium, through their number, by which the preacher in charge can always control a Quarterly Conference. The increase in the legal numbers of the stewards is an interesting study. Beginning with two, Conference after Conference has extended the legal limit, until, by act of the General Conference of 1884, the numbers are fixed at three and thirteen, an increase of four over the act of 1872.

Second: The composition of the Conference was an inevitable result of the peculiar character of the early ministry of the church. Beginning almost exclusively in evangelistic and circuit work, the persons with whom the preacher naturally came into contact, and with whom he would counsel, were the local preachers and exhorters, the right arms of the itinerants of that early day; the class-leaders, as knowing the religious state of the members; and the stewards, who gathered the contributions of the people. These men were a necessity to the successful work of the ministry. There was the more reason to form them into an official body, because they generally represented the most useful of the members, and those best fitted for service.

The power given to a pastor to control a Quarterly Conference through his right of nomination and appointment was unquestionably due to a belief that such authority was required to secure the most suitable members for the several places. At the same time it carried out the policy of the church by placing all power in the ministry.

While it is acknowledged that the Quarterly Conference cannot, in some form, be dispensed with, yet the question now is, whether it is, under the present conditions and circumstances of the church, necessary or advisable (1) to continue the controlling power of the ministry over it, and (2) to retain the present composition of a body charged with its peculiar duties.

That there should be some body with authority to take care of and conduct the spiritual and temporal interests of each circuit or station in harmony with the duties of the Annual, and the power of the General Conference, is evident. How such a body should be constituted, and where the power necessary to its success should be placed, are important questions, the answers to which will be judged by their tendency to increase the efficiency of the individual station or circuit, and by the greater acceptability of the plan to the laity.

The first requisite of any plan would be to free it from the control of the minister in charge. The second, to make it a body truly representative of the membership.

An objection to the continuance of the power exercised over the Quarterly Conference by the preacher in charge is, that it is not needed to secure the proper attention to the business of the church; and as power should only be given when required for certain purposes, therefore the power now given to the preacher over the Quarterly Conference is unwise, and should be withdrawn. Another objection is to be found in the fact that through this power the minister controls the purse as well as the pulpit of the church. The possession of such a control is dangerous to the ministry and to the laity. Such a union is wrong in theory and principle; it is bad in practice. To take care of the spiritual interests of the church is the special work of the pastor. It embraces enough to employ all his time and talents.

It may be well, at this point, to notice a difficulty that will be met by any suggestions for change, either in the composition of the Quarterly Conference or in the laws regulating it.

The ministry have been from the first intimately connected with the management of every interest of their appointments; they have generally carried the burdens that come with the financial needs as well as the spiritual interests of their churches. Indeed, it has so largely become their habit to look after the condition of the treasury, that with difficulty they keep themselves from interfering even when there is no necessity for it. In this respect their work resembles most closely that of the Catholic priest, and is unlike that of the ministers of the other churches. It had its origin in the fact of the early preachers being so thoroughly evangelists. They had to provide for and take care of their personal necessities. This interference with the business of the charges has continued to the present day. A Methodist preacher accepts it as part of his work.

The form of the Quarterly Conference is objectionable in that it does not provide for a proper representation of the members of any station or circuit, and thereby deprives them of the control of the business and finances of the circuits and stations.

This is a more serious objection than may at first sight appear, because there is no way by which a layman may become a member of the Quarterly Conference other than through the preacher in charge. This is true even in States where the law requires that trustees must be elected by the members of the church, because they are, when elected, subject to the approval of the Quarterly Conference. A Quarterly Conference is no more a representative body of a church than a

Congress would be of the people of the United States if its members were composed solely of persons appointed by the President, and of others nominated by him and approved by persons he had appointed. Men of unexceptionable character, acquirements, and piety may be members of the church for thirty, forty, or sixty years without being members of this official body, if for any reason they have failed to meet the approval or to get the favor of the preacher in charge. Whereas a member of a church who has at one time, and in some other charge, been elected an exhorter or a local preacher; a minister who has become supernumerary, from whatever cause, or superannuated; a class-leader who may continue in charge of a class, are members of the Quarterly Conference so long as such relations continue. To argue that a body so exclusive, so appointed,—a body that is not responsible to the immediate church for the conduct of its secular business,—is representative, is an absurdity.

There is no reason, in the nature of the case, why class-leaders, exhorters, local and attached supernumerary and superannuated preachers, Sunday-school superintendents, or trustees should be members, by virtue of their position, of such a body. The purpose for which a Quarterly Conference exists in the church can be reached without this exclusiveness, violation, and perversion of the representative principle. This body should be chosen by the members; it might be divided into two bodies,—one having charge of the spiritual, the other of the secular interests of a church. If, as is often the case, the class-leaders, exhorters, local ministers, Sunday-school superintendents, and trustees of a church are the better qualified to be members of the Quarterly Conference, they will be chosen by the members of a station. The attached ministers of a Conference have no proper claim or right either to a place, a vote, or a representation in the Quarterly Conference. Why should they vote on the secular business of a church of which they are not members, and to the support of which they may not be contributors? The present method of constituting a Quarterly Conference may prevent, as has been noticed, the use of the best talent and most marked piety in a church. The members are the best judges of the suitability of their brethren for places in such a body.

Another objection is the general one, which will be frequently noted, that the present plan is injurious to all parties, because it places upon the ministry duties which are not in harmony with their peculiar work; because it separates them from the body of the members; because it prevents the members from partaking as fully as they should feel it is their right and duty to do in the management of the interests of the individual church, and they are thereby the losers in grace from failing to do their whole duty; because these hindrances to the individual churches affect in the aggregate the prosperity of the whole church, and by so doing interfere with its highest duty,—the conversion of the people. To the appointments by the minister of the spiritual leaders and teachers in the church, viz., the class-leaders and the Sunday-school superintendents, there should be no objection, nor to the presence of the pastor as a member of the Quarterly Conference, nor to the presidency of the elder. It is acknowledged that, as a whole, the pastors have used their power over the Quarterly Conference with great prudence, and it is largely owing to this fact that the laity have not taken more decided action in favor of changes in the church organizations which would be in harmony with the spirit of the country and the welfare of the church. The hand of power has pressed lightly upon them, though not less absolute when exerted.

Finally, the duties of a Quarterly Conference could be as well done by an elected, and therefore a representative body, as they are now by the appointed body. They could attend to all the financial wants of the church or circuit, provide for the support of the ministers, of the presiding elder, take care of the property of the church, plan for its extension, give and renew licenses of exhorters and local preachers, and pass judgment on applicants for the ministry. There are no duties of a Conference, which are now performed by the brethren who are appointed, that the same brethren could not perform if they were elected by the membership.

The election of representatives to the lay Conference should be reserved to the members at large, and not given to any smaller body. An objection to the election of such delegates by the Quarterly Conference, apart from the principle, is found in the fact that a minister, through his power of appointment of members of the Conference, can, in many cases, determine the selection of such representatives, and the lay Conferences are thereby unduly and improperly influenced by the ministry. All such possibilities and temptations should be removed from the ministry; they have temptations enough, growing out of the performance of their proper duties.

An important point will be gained in broadening the members by increasing their interest in and knowledge of the workings of the church through the introduction of such changes in the Quarterly Conference as shall make it a representative body, freed from the domination of the preacher in charge. The ministerial brethren need not be alarmed by these suggestions; if adopted they will greatly relieve them from responsibilities they should not have. Nor need they fear the introduction of elections by the members; these can be held with as little commotion and as little friction as is now present in the election of trustees as provided by the laws of some States. They may be assured that the laity will not disgrace themselves with the electioneering tactics which are quadrennially used in some of the Annual and General Conferences.

LOCAL PREACHERS AND EXHORTERS.

Before closing this analysis and review of the institution, work, and constitution of the Quarterly Conference, it may be advisable to look more carefully at one of its distinguishing features, viz., the local preachers*

---

* The Annual Conferences have power to locate or place in the ranks of local preachers members of the Annual Conferences. They then become responsible to the Quarterly Conference to which they are attached.

and exhorters, who are created by and are responsible to the Quarterly Conference.

As a part of the organism of the Methodist Episcopal Church this relation deserves some study. The presence of such officers in the church is one of its peculiarities; they, with the pastor and class-leaders, form a spiritual quartette that has been a power for good in the church. The early preachers appointed by Mr. Wesley, like the "poor priests" or itinerant preachers of Wycliffe, went about their work to instruct the people in a knowledge of the gospel. They, too, were denounced "As unauthorized itinerant preachers, who set forth erroneous, yea, heretical assertions in public sermons, not only in churches, but also in public squares and other profane places, and who do this under the guise of great holiness, but without having obtained any Episcopal or Papal authorization." (Archbishop Courtenay to Bishop of London, 1382.)

After the introduction of ordination into the church, the office of local preacher was continued for local purposes in England, and was made a like part of the organization of the church in this country. In the early days these preachers were useful in supplying the pulpits, in the absence of the circuit preacher and in opening new places for religious service; their work was a continuation of the more purely evangelistic labor of the earlier preachers. Through this office the gifts and graces of many men have been developed, and their way opened into the itinerancy; this relation to the church was also held by many who withdrew from the active ministry.

It will be readily comprehended wherein the work of a local preacher was and is advantageous to the church, on large circuits in newly-settled districts of country, and in more settled places where openings may still be found for missions or for the initiation of churches; yet, in the older territory of the church, there seems but little place for the local ministry or for the exhorters. The last two General Conferences were impressed with the necessity that more care should be taken by the Quarterly and District Conferences in admitting candidates for local preachers' licenses, and therefore increased the subjects on which they are to be examined when applying for orders. This is a step in the right direction, and needs to be closely followed up by increasing the requirements and decreasing the numbers.

The necessity for their existence is rapidly fading away because of their general unacceptability as preachers, their failure to do the special work that the office was created for, the lack of care of Quarterly Conferences in selecting for preachers men of intelligence and of accepted and acknowledged religious character, and further, because the work they did in former times can now be done without the authority of church appointment, which was then thought necessary. This is another evidence of the change in the theology of the church as to the peculiar right of the ministers to teach and preach publicly. The right of the laity to speak and teach without formal appointment is generally recognized.

The proof is at hand that, in addition to the failure

to perform their whole duty, there are many more in the local ranks than are required. This proof is found in a recent circular of the Home Mission Society of the Methodist Episcopal Church in Philadelphia, which says in effect that there are in that city two hundred local preachers (or about two to each church), that the majority of them are doing but little in their official capacity, and an appeal is made to the church to furnish money to find these two hundred men, or a majority of them, something to do. This is practically confessing that the evangelistic spirit has departed from the local preachers as a body or they would find plenty of work in a large city, and, as there are few vacant pulpits for them to fill, owing to the abundance of supernumeraries, their usefulness is about at an end. As it is in the city of Philadelphia, so it probably is in all the more settled parts of the country.

Another thought is worth remembering, that the fact of holding authority to preach operates against the influence and acceptability of these brethren. The authorized preacher comes with an endorsement of the church, which is received as assuring a fair degree of ability and acquirements, and, as the great majority of the local preachers fail to reach the lowest standard, they are unacceptable. The layman may preach no better, yet will be more acceptable, because he comes with no profession or endorsement of ability. So long as the newer country may need the services of local preachers and exhorters, it might not be prudent to dispense with the office. It may be necessary to continue the relation as a home, a resting-place, for the travelling ministers when they lose their efficiency or become supernumerary, or by time and infirmities superannuated, unless the church should accept the suggestion hereinbefore made, that such men who are worthy may be continued as members of the ministry of the church at large, without being members of an Annual Conference. Yet some plan should be devised to reduce the number of local preachers and prevent such misuse of their office as seems to exist in the city of Philadelphia.

The local preachers as a body feel that they are like a fifth wheel to a wagon, and that there is now no proper place for them in church work. They do not seem to understand the causes which have been operating to produce this result, and are making vain efforts to magnify their office by securing some more distinctly recognized position of influence in the church. They do not see that they have as a body either failed to do their work well, and therefore cannot have any higher position, or that, owing to the development and growth of the church in all directions, there is no demand for their services. Still, a higher grade of men, lessened numbers, and deeper piety might contribute to make the office of local preacher more useful and acceptable to the people. The office of exhorter is entirely unnecessary.

CHAPTER III.

The defects and dangers arising from the constitution and form of management of the charitable work of the church, and of its publishing interests.

HAVING thus fully analyzed and discussed the three councils of the church, the second class of subjects is to be examined, viz., the official charitable work and the publishing interests of the church.

FIRST: THE OFFICIAL CHARITABLE WORK OF THE CHURCH.

When the laity open the Discipline to gain information upon the structure of the official charitable organizations of the church, they will *first* be surprised to find how imperfectly they are described, the Board of Church Extension being the only one that is properly and intelligently presented. The *second* defect will be found in the inconsistency in the titles of many of these organizations. They are known by the names of the Missionary Society, the Board of Church Extension, the Sunday-School Union, the Freedmen's Aid Society, the Tract Society, and the Board of Education.

Many of the laity will be surprised to find that there is no society, in fact, connected with any of these boards, the General Conference of 1872 having taken action which did away with every vestige of a society and placed the control of these interests in managers appointed by the General Conference. As to the provision for auxiliary societies found in the Discipline, the question will be asked, How can a society be auxiliary to a board? And as to life-membership, patrons, etc., of these boards, there would be as much relevancy if they were connected with the obelisk in the New York Central Park.

The *third* result will be equally new to most of the laity: that there is now no responsibility connected with any of these boards to the church or to the members; that no contributor has a vote, or by his membership in an auxiliary society, any influence in their management. If a contributor insists that his local society must be auxiliary to a society, as the Discipline has it, he is informed that it is auxiliary to a board, which merely means that the local society is to send its contributions to the board to be by it distributed.

The *fourth* point is in the manner of the constitution of these boards. The laity who have not examined this subject will be astonished to find how shrewdly an apparent fairness in equal clerical and lay representation in the boards is turned into an impotent minority of the laity, and how thoroughly the way is guarded, in their formation, to keep the power in the hands of the clergy.

Before showing how the boards are constructed it will be well to look more closely at the changes made in the church societies by the act of the General Conference of 1872.

The object of forming societies to carry on church work is twofold: First, to procure by charter the right to receive bequests, to make contracts, and to carry on the work without the managers incurring any personal liability; and, secondly, to increase the interest in, and pecuniary aid to, the different causes by a personal membership. The influence of such membership on the personal and active interest taken needs no argument. This power for good is used by nearly all the churches. The Roman Catholics understand and use it extensively in their work. The influence of it is seen in the interest in the annual meetings of the "American Board;" in the missionary work of the Wesleyans, and most fully in that of the "Women's Foreign Missionary Society of the Methodist Episcopal Church." In these instances the society in each individual church feels that it is part of the principal body, and that it is doing a special work. Three reasons may be given for the success of the last-named society: First, in that it adopts thoroughly the society idea; secondly, in that it is the only society in the church in which the members have any direct interest, representation, or influence; and, thirdly, in that the contributors are furnished a detailed account of the expenditures. There is not now much encouragement to our members to make contributions to causes over which they have no control; in whose management they have no representation; whose policy they have no opportunity to discuss or to influence, nor knowledge as to how their money is expended. But further than this, while the lay contributors have no voice in the distribution of their money, there is no provision in the law of the church or of these boards which requires that the managers—the men who distribute the money—should have given one penny to any of these causes. Herein is a great error. Money qualification, as determinative of the interest felt in proportion to one's means, should be a test of the right of representation; however small the contribution might be, the principle should be recognized. The Wesleyan Mission Society permits every annual subscriber of one pound to take part in certain meetings of the society.

When an arbitrarily formed body makes a demand on the members of a church for aid in any cause, much of the strength of the demand is lost by a sense of unfairness and the want of responsibility in the body making the demand. Yet in compliance with the wish, as it was understood, of the clique of office-holders at 805 Broadway, New York, the General Conference of 1872 adopted the plan of boards of managers, to be appointed by the Conference, in place of managers elected by the societies, to conduct their affairs, ostensibly for the purpose of bringing these societies "into organic union with the church, instead of being under the uncertain control of members made such by voluntary contributions." (Tract No. 4, Society Series.) The real object was to get rid of any possible opposition by the laity to the absolute control of these societies by the ministers of the church. There had been no uncertainty in the control of the societies by the contributing members. These societies had never injured the causes they represented; indeed, the interest of the church in the causes was created through the societies thus abolished. The contributors were loyal to the church. But as the contributors to these societies were the laity, and the fact of such contribution made them members, with all the rights of such to partake in their management, in determining their policy, and in electing the officers, such rights and powers were considered an interference with the higher right of the ministers to manage the church. The change from societies to boards thus introduced a direct charge that the laity of the church were unreliable, and could not be trusted with the management of such interests. It was an insult to their Christian manhood. The argument for "closer organic union" was a miserable apology for so great a wrong, and even if such union were desirable, it was obtained at too great a cost. This violently taking out of the hands of the laity the control of the charities of the church, without notice to the members of the societies, and placing them almost absolutely under the control of the ministry, was a great wrong, not only to the laity and the church, but to the cause of Jesus Christ, and was followed by other acts of questionable character. In obedience to the action of the General Conference, applications were made to the legislatures of several States by some societies regularly, and by others irregularly, for changes in their charters; transferring the management to boards appointed by the General Conference. The amendments thus made involved serious questions of their constitutionality. The invasion of private and vested rights, the violation of contracts, the fraud on the States, in securing a grant of corporate powers to irresponsible boards, are questions which might have been raised at an earlier day. But by reason of the peculiar work of these boards, the absence of danger from them to the public weal, and the time that has elapsed, any court would be tempted to condone the wrong. That which would not be permitted in private or corporate relations between men, because of wrong, can be allowed to the church, on the principle that the church may be pardoned for doing wrong if good shall come of it.

So much as to this change from societies under the control of the laity to boards under the control of the ministers has been written, not in expectation of any reversal of the policy of boards, but to show how carefully the ministers have guarded every point in the organization of the church so as to prevent the laity from having any influence in its legislation, and further to show to the laity the danger there is in leaving the control of these interests in the hands of the ministry. The boards of managers of all the general societies, so called, are appointed by the General Conference in this wise: Previous to the General Conference of 1884 the Board of Bishops submitted names of managers of the several boards to the approval of the General Conference. But in 1884 it was discovered that this power was too great to be trusted to the bishops, and a new plan was adopted, which would place such nominations under the control of the ministry. The General Conference elects its standing committees, in which the laity are in the minority; the standing committees elect their chairmen; the ministers, being in a majority, can always secure the chairman. The bishops, numbering twelve, with the twelve chairmen of the standing committees (of which, in May, 1884, nine were ministers and three laymen), nominate the managers of the boards, equally divided between the ministry and the laity, subject to the approval of the General Conference. That is, a committee of twenty-one ministers and three laymen make the managers of the boards of all our great benevolent institutions. But, as a *fifth* point, the more thoroughly to control these charities, another ministerial wheel connected with the more important of these boards, viz., the Missionary and Church Extension, comes into use. There is a committee termed the General Committee of the Missionary Society, and one for the Board of Church Extension. The committee in the case of the Missionary Society, which may be used as an example, is composed of the bishops (twelve), the members of the General Conference districts (thirteen, all ministers), a committee of twelve of the board of managers (six laymen and six ministers), with the corresponding secretaries (two) and the treasurers (two), making in all thirty-four ministers to seven laymen. It is the duty of this committee to meet annually, and to determine what fields shall be occupied as foreign missions, the number of persons to be employed, the amount of money required for the support of the missions; it regulates domestic missions, and assesses the church in sums to meet all expenses.

The board of managers merely carry out the will of the general mission committee; they act as an executive committee, and for all practical purposes their number might be decreased to the present number of one of their sub-committees. The treasurers of the Missionary Society are the Book Agents,—one in New York and one in Cincinnati. With the exception of Mr. Phillips they have always been ministers. The laity will now understand how completely all the charities of the church are controlled by the ministers, and will ask, Was there any necessity for the change from the societies to the boards? Was there any good reason for this purposed exclusion of the laity? Is it not an unjust, unsafe, and unscriptural division of responsibility? Should not those who contribute the money have an equal voice in its distribution? Should the great interests involving the appropriation and disbursement of much more than a million of dollars annually be so absolutely under the control of the ministers? Are there not elements of danger in it to the ministry and the church? Is not the hearty co-operation of the laity a necessity to success? The laity will ask in loud tones if it is not high time that such control should end. They will point to the comparatively small contributions of the church as an evidence that a radical change is needed. These boards, as constituted, do not and cannot reach the hearts and pockets of the laity to the extent the causes demand. The laity are kept at a distance, and know little about them except as they are yearly informed of the assessments these magnates in Zion have imposed upon them. No amount of pulpit or oratorical ability or persuasive talent which these boards can employ will make up for the want of knowledge and personal interest felt by the laity of the church. The ministers have failed to see the cause of their failure; they should learn that the laity are no longer children to be kept in leading-strings. If proper success is to be had in the mission, church extension, and other work of the church, the laity must be made responsible by having a full share in the management. They understand what the members want to know, and they have the ability to reach them. Whatever may be the best policy as to church boards or societies, one thing is a prerequisite to success,—that there must be an approximation to a fair representation of the laity in these boards. In accordance with the principles already discussed, such boards should consist of representatives of the membership of the church (including the ministry), without regard to their order. A reasonable suggestion would be to select as managers of the boards from two-thirds to three-fourths from the lay members and the one-third or one-fourth from the ministers.

There are many good reasons for making some distinction in the proportion. Among them are the facts that, as the secretaries are and will probably be ministers, they affiliate with men of the same class in the boards. They hang together and defend each other. Their class feeling and jealousy of the interference of laymen are quickly excited. All laymen who have been members of boards of managers in any religious or church society understand what this class feeling means, and how thoroughly it operates to prevent proper examination of finances, of management, and of policy, more especially if the secretary if a minister is in any way involved in the examination or discussion. They further know how such conduct tends to lower the confidence of the laity in the ministers, because they fail to measure up to the high standard they teach. Then, again, there is among the ministerial representatives in such boards a constant tendency to extravagance in salaries and expenses. Not being accustomed to the use of money in large amounts, they use it badly; not being trained to business accuracy, their accounts are generally loosely prepared, and they lack care and knowledge in investments. In fact, their education and habits as ministers do and should unfit them for the business work of such boards. Then, again, there can be no denial of the proposition so often made in these pages, that the parties having the largest interest should have the controlling power, and in harmony with this, the laity being the principal contributors, in numbers and in money, should have a decidedly preponderating influence in determining the distribution of the money.

If, then, in view of these arguments, and conceding the force of habit, the laity should insist upon an equal division of the membership of the different boards between the ministry and laity, they would be asking but little and yielding much. Let, then, the laity insist on equal representation on all boards, on all committees, and on the joint executive or general committees of the Missionary and Church Extension Boards. Let them insist that full and accurate reports shall be made of the proceedings of the boards; of the reception and expenditure of the money; of salaries paid, incidental expenses, etc.; of the results obtained; of the providential openings for new and increased work, and all other information by which the members may be educated in the history and progress of each charity. If this were done the younger members of the church would acquire a deeper interest in each cause, the collections would increase, by the responsibility placed upon the laity to take their part in the management, and to give their counsel, as well as their money.

These remarks are applicable to all the boards. The large amounts heretofore given to them are a mark of the general confidence of the church in their management. But from the "Church Extension" Board there has not for years been an intelligible report by which the laity could measure the economy or the success of the management. No proper account of expenses has been rendered, of the distribution of the money received, of the money invested or loaned, or of the churches to which it has been loaned, the length of time, amount unpaid, interest due, amounts suspended or cancelled or lost. Nor has it been stated how much of yearly contributions has been applied to making good the interest on the amounts loaned and the principal of the loans. Nor has information been given of the terms of the annuities, including probable duration, rate of interest, and amount loaned, the character of the property received, whether money or real estate, and the liabilities of the board.

There has been in connection with this society a most reprehensible practice by which to increase its loan fund, viz., the securing of devises in wills, or grants of property under an agreement to pay annuities; a simple repetition of the policy of the Roman Catholic Church which has been condemned by the courts and legislatures of the States, as taking advantage of weakness of mind and of the disposition of old age to purchase happiness hereafter. When the membership in the General Conference shall be equally divided between the ministry and the laity, and when the *personnel* of the boards of managers is readjusted (and such a time must be waited for, because of the difficulty the laity always meet in introducing investigations into the plan and the management of religious societies which are controlled by the ministry), then one of the questions to be discussed will be this institution of loan and annuity funds by our boards. The laity will inquire, First: Into the legal power to accept and hold such funds under their charters, unless they come under all the provisions introduced by legislatures in Annuity Company Charters, with a proper capital for the protection of the persons interested, and are made subject to taxation and the supervision of the courts. The laity will at once see that in the Church Extension Board there is no capital, and no financial responsibility; no security for the investors. Its being a church institution would in such matters operate against rather than in its favor. Second: The laity would start the query and accompany it with an answer, that if the purpose of introducing such a financial business was to make money out of it, then it is wrong; for the church has no business to enter into any scheme for the object of financial profit.

Third: That if the object be to get the best results of the money, to secure the greatest safety, then such money should be placed in charge of some company chartered for such a purpose. Prudent investment of money requires the employment of trained men, who are used to examination of titles, who understand the laws of real and personal estate, values of property, condition of the money market, and many other points. What fitness is there in intrusting to a benevolent body, under church control, with a majority of ministers in its management, with a minister at its head, such duties, involving the care of such investments? The argument that such funds are used to help poor churches is an evidence of the insecurity of the investments. Few capitalists will loan money on churches, unless well secured in the value of the property and by personal bonds. No prudent man, as a business operation, would lend money for a length of time to a church that is poor in any sense. The private citizen may prosecute his claim to a sale, the Church Board cannot. The fact of the loan being made by a Church Board is an evidence that it is attended by great risk and probable loss, and in the absence of any danger of sale, the loan is unpaid, interest accumulates, to be ultimately forgiven.

If individuals choose to institute a fund for such purposes, for which there is no responsibility except honesty in permanently investing it, there can be no objection; but for a church society to invest funds on which it has to pay a fixed annuity will be conceded to be a most unwise policy. Fourth: The laity will also discover that the only method of meeting any deficiency in such receipts, or of making good any money lost through bad loans or imprudent investments, is by use of moneys contributed by the members for other purposes. Such engagements under the annuity system by any of the boards is placing a responsibility upon the church that is wrong, and that the laity will refuse to recognize. Fifth: The laity will further make note that in this increase of financial operations, which are not in themselves necessary, there is involved much of risk to the church, the secretaries, the managers, and to the parties financially interested; that it adds to the number of offices to be filled; that it offers tempting places to the ministry; that it creates sinecures; and is demoralizing and dangerous in its results. Sixth: That there is a tendency to increase society investments in this line was proven by the introduction of a plan in the last General Conference to add the powers of a Fire Insurance Company to those of an Annuity Life Insurance in the Board of Church Extension. Fortunately and with some degree of surprise, the proposition did not meet with favor. There must be a total disseverance of plans of money-making from those of saving immortal souls.*

The history of church boards and societies teaches us how great care should be constantly taken to confine their operations to proper church work; to secure economy of working; to keep them from becoming

---

* Recent developments in the management of the Church Extension Society justify and enforce the above criticisms.

merely soft places with good salaries; to make them effective, and to prevent fraud and loss. The presence of a large number of educated and independent business men in these boards is necessary to secure such results. There is danger in them if this is not done. A final recommendation is in place. In the analysis of the General Conference it was suggested, as a preventive against the evils arising from electioneering for office, with its questionable accompaniments, and as a means of securing men better fitted for the different offices, that the boards of managers, when properly constituted, by the admission of the laity, should have the selection of their executive officers, and that in such selection they should be guided by the principle of assigning to a minister such duties as properly belong to his "calling," and to a layman such duties as appertain to matters of business. The advantages of a division of labor would be seen in the improved working of the Missionary Board and of the Board of Church Extension.

PUBLISHING INTERESTS.

One of the first duties that will devolve upon the laity, when properly represented in the General Conference, will be to make a thorough examination of the policy of the publishing business of the church, including the methods of management, supervision, and how far these should be continued, enlarged, or diminished. It may be said, generally, that all money matters are sources of temptation to the individual in the church as well as in trade, and that these temptations and the accompanying evils increase just as the necessity for such operations by a church diminishes. Failure is very apt to follow a man who late in life changes his business. Any money engagement of an individual minister or of a church that is not strictly within the limits of propriety and necessity will corrupt and injure both the man and the church. The black roll is not small of Methodist ministers who have been led into speculation and lost their money, and with it their religion and reputation. Will not the result be the same with larger operations?

An examination of the object and management of the publishing interests of the Methodist Episcopal Church may be timely, and if there is any source of danger or any cause to fear injury to the church or the ministry, it may appear and be suggestive of required changes or increased guards.

The publishing interests originated at an early day in the history of the church; it was thought by the Fathers, and it was probably true, that they were at that time necessary, in order that our members might be supplied with its own literature. As in the case of John Wesley, publishers could not be found who would take the risk of publishing Methodist books, and booksellers would not keep them on their shelves. As a result of these difficulties in the way of reaching the people, the publication of books was commenced and their distribution and sale secured through the travelling preachers. To satisfy the members that the object of such publication was not to make personal profit, and to avoid the dangers arising from accumulated capital, it was provided that all surplus profits should be divided among the Conferences, to be applied to aid the needy ministers. Both objects were good in their day, but the management of these interests has gone far beyond the simple principles on which they were started. The questions are, How far, or to what extent, under the changed conditions of business, of the church, and of the country, such publishing establishments are now required by the church? Is the money annually distributed (in 1884 some fifteen thousand dollars to the Annual Conferences) of any material help to the needy? To answer the last question first, the amount distributed is so small that it probably (as will be shown hereafter) takes more from them, in the way of aid from the laity, than it contributes. If this is so, the petty distribution is an evil; and, further, if the small pittance per head is used as an argument to uphold the continuance of the publishing interests of the church as now carried on, though contrary to its welfare, then they are a temptation to wrong, are demoralizing to the ministry, and a danger to the church. In considering our publishing policy, this matter of distribution of surplus profits should be thrown out of the account.

There are certain principles which will be acknowledged by every one as determinative of the extent of such undertakings, the character of publications, and the make-up of the superintendence. The object of the church in the publication of books, reviews, and printing newspapers, tracts, Sunday-school journals, etc., was,—

First: To secure to its people a supply of such literature as it deemed essential to their Christian education, and in harmony with its doctrines and usages.

Second: To bring the cost of its publications to the lowest figures consistent with pecuniary safety, in order to meet the means of its members and to secure the largest circulation.

Third: To secure for the management of such interests men experienced in the business, and a proper supervisory control of the management and the character of the publications.

Fourth: To restrict the capital invested to the needs of the business.

Fifth: That annual reports of the operations, the results, and the condition of such publishing operations should be issued for the information of the members.

Sixth: All these principles grow out of and are subordinate to the general principle that the church of Christ is intended to take care of the spiritual wants of man, and therefore should be, as far as possible, separated from secular interests, more especially those of the lower order, such as the making and holding of money.

Without entering into any argument as to how far the action of the Book Agents during the past four or more years harmonizes with such principles, yet by a series of interrogatories some of the points in question may be more forcibly brought before the church.

First: Does the church, through its agents, confine its publications to those books, papers, tracts, etc., which are essential to the education of its people as Christians, and which would not be furnished at as low prices by the book-making trade? A glance at the catalogues of the two Book Concerns will answer this question. If these catalogues were subjected to the tests named they would not require many pages to cover their publications.

Second: How does the cost of publication compare with that of the trade? While it is true that a mere majority of a sub-committee of the Book Committee in February, 1884,* reported favorably upon this question, yet two suggestions as to the value of their report will come up.

First: This majority of the sub-committee was composed of two ministers and two laymen, who, with great care and to the extent of their knowledge and ability, made the best examination they could, but no member of the committee had any practical knowledge of the business. A sufficient answer to the conclusions of their report is, that it was not the kind of committee that a silent partner in such houses as Harper & Brothers, Lippincott's, or Appleton's would have selected to examine into the economy of the management of their business.

Second: Such a result is contrary to the experience and judgment of all business men, which teaches that there are not the same inducements to energy and economy in a church institution, with two millions of readers, and a monopoly of a large class of publications, as the individual publisher has, who com-

---

* See report of minority of the sub-committee published in the *Daily Christian Advocate*, May 6, 1884.

petes in the open market for the sale of his productions. Is not this also proven by the fact that other publishers will make better terms with popular Methodist authors than the Book Agents? Is it, then, any wonder that it is said by men who understand the business, that the publications of the Book Concern are not furnished to the church at as low prices as they might be? The management of the publishing interests of the Methodist Episcopal Church is not singular in this respect. The same facts are believed to be true as to the cost of the publications of the American Bible Society, the Presbyterian Board, the Baptist Publication Society, the Sunday-School Union, and the American Tract Society. The difficulty is inherent in the use of paid agents without competent supervision.

Third: What moral right has the church to enter into a general publishing business as a money-making operation; and even more than this, to enter into competition with private printers for job work? The Western Book Agents reported to the General Conference of 1884 that in the previous four years they had done nearly three hundred thousand dollars' worth of such work, with the excuse that the profits on it cheapened the cost of regular publications. It is understood that the New York agents do no work for others. The laity will ask, Is this right? Has the ministry fallen so low as to hunt up job work and take it away from some hard-working man in the business, who is striving to raise his family and train them in righteousness? The laity will also ask, Is it requisite in order to secure Methodist literature, that the agents should go outside of church wants and enter into the general work of publishers as well as of job printers? Must they violate the broad principles of right and propriety that a few pennies may be saved in the cost of a book, or that the worn-out preacher may realize a part of a penny more in his annual dole? Are not the members of the church able and willing to pay for church literature its cost when the business is conducted on Christian principles?

So far as the principle is involved, could not the General Conference, for the church, as well enter into the dry-goods business in competition with Messrs. Arnold, Constable & Co., into the iron business in competition with Messrs. J. B. & J. M. Cornell, into the Atlantic steamship business in competition with the North German Lloyd Company, or into the cheap clothing business in competition with the Bowery Jew?

Fourth: The question will be asked, With a joint capital in the two Book Concerns of $1,607,450.30, would not the interests of the church be promoted by a union of the two Concerns in New York and Cincinnati? Would not such union increase the possible economies and lessen the losses and the capital required to carry on the business? If the united interests were kept within proper bounds in the character of their publications and work, would not much less capital be required? If the work now done under the different agents were done by contract, could not this capital be yet further reduced, and the surplus divided among the needy ministers? Is it necessary and prudent that the church should own such large amounts of real estate in the cities of New York and Cincinnati?

Amounting in New York to $682,250
"   " Cincinnati to 299,000
Making a total of $981,250

What defence can there be for placing the Book Agents' office in a building at 805 Broadway, New York, costing nearly one million of dollars, while the great book-store of Methodism occupies the cellar?

The board of the Missionary Society, of the Sunday-School Union, the editor of the *Quarterly Review*, and the book-room agents and other officers, could be accommodated quite as well in rooms that would cost very much less money, and thereby enable the agents to elevate their salesroom to a ground-floor, not on Broadway, which is accepted as being no longer a desirable location for a retail book-store, but to place it in a suitable building in the vicinity of the leading book-houses. Such a change would contribute to increase the business and profits and thereby decrease the losses which, it is understood, are now incurred in the retail department of the Book Concern. If the ambition of the New York ministry and laity demands such a grand property as 805 Broadway, let them pay for it; the members of the church should not be called on to contribute. A very striking evidence of the bad management of these agencies is in their valuation of the amount due them for sales. The New York agents report (1883) that on an amount of credits of $378,883.77 they expect to lose twenty per cent., or $75,766.75. Such losses would ruin any publishing-house in the trade. Then, again, if it were not for these losses, the profit for 1883 would have been $152,946.10, or twelve and seven-tenths per cent. on its capital of $1,202,593.07. These figures affect only the New York office. The same general facts probably exist in the Western agency. The system of using depositories or branch book-stores in other cities has been not only unnecessary and a source of almost continued expense, but such stores have interfered with the sale of our books in the general market, and thereby have been in antagonism with an important duty of the church, and one object of the creation of the Book Concerns, viz., the general dissemination of books explaining and defending our doctrines, polity, and usages, including our general literature, among the people. This exclusion tends to force Methodist authors to seek other publishers than the Book Agents. These suggestions and criticisms, taken together, demonstrate the need of a thorough purging in the management of the Book Concerns, and the necessity of employing competent men to take charge of them.

As to the character of the management of these interests, the laity will quickly decide that whatever may be the extent of the publishing operations of the church, and as their management will have to be through agents, it will be policy and economy to secure as agents men who are qualified for the places by education and business training. The figures just given demonstrate this necessity. The laymen well understand that the proper superintendency of such a business requires two grades of ability,—the one the required practical knowledge of the book trade and manufacture, and the other business tact, ability to manage finances, and a good judgment of the literary wants of the church.

The laity will also ask, What peculiar propriety is there in electing an effective travelling preacher as an agent to fill either of these positions? It is understood why this was done at an early day, but why should it be done now, when talent and acquirements of all kinds are so abundant? The simple fact is, the church has not thought about it. The force of habit has continued the early practice, and the ministry will not intervene, for the places are considered desirable for profit, influence, and honor.

When the laity look into the question, they will find that the duties of the agents are purely secular, and therefore that the agency is no place for an effective minister, called to preach Christ and him crucified; that the theological questions are referred to the editor of the *Quarterly Review* and the secretary of the Sunday-School Union as literary experts; that the demand of the church or of the market for books can be better understood by a layman brought up in the trade than by a preacher. That there is no law of need which requires that an agent should be a preacher is proven by the fact that the church has had for a number of years, and now has, one layman as agent in New York. They will note the fact that in the trade the publishers of law-books are not lawyers, nor of medical works, doctors, nor of scientific books, doctors of philosophy, nor of works in the ancient and modern languages, professors of languages, nor of literary works, authors, nor of theological works, ministers. Successful publishers require rare talent in dealing with authors and acuteness in understanding the wants of the market. They employ experts or proficients in the several departments to examine manuscript and to edit books. Therefore there is no reason why, primarily, effective ministers should be chosen as agents.

The next question the laity will inquire into is the fitness of an applicant for the place of agent. This is a fair question and will harm no one, for men are not elected to office without their consent and desire. They will ask as to his knowledge of the practical part of the business, his experience with men, his habits of economy. They will also ask as to his peculiar fitness for the general duties of a publisher; how great has been his experience; in what house he was raised; the judgment of those who have been associated with him in business. If it should happen that an effective travelling preacher possesses the required qualifications and has misinterpreted his call, let him first accept a local relation and then be elected.

If the General Conferences had asked these questions in the past twenty years, how many of the agents would have failed of an election! yet every layman will agree as to their propriety.

The qualifications of proper agents will suggest to the laity the incompetency of a General Conference to judiciously select them by a majority vote. Common sense dictates that they should be chosen by the Book Committee, and that this committee should be carefully selected for the peculiar fitness of its members for their duties, without regard to territorial boundaries or Conference districts; and further, that this committee should consist principally of laymen, with enough of the ministerial element to keep their theology safe with the aid of the literary experts. By adopting these suggestions the publishing interests of the church would be brought within safe limits and better results be secured, while the church would be saved from the dangers that accompany the admixture of spiritual matters with the secular object of making money.

There is another matter of interest to the church connected with this habit of electing ministers as agents which may be referred to here, but will be more fully treated hereafter; it is found in its influence on the ministers and on the church.

The office of Book Agent is in itself a temptation to many men to leave the ministry. If they are useful ministers the church cannot spare them from the pulpit; and if they are not useful or have lost their usefulness, then they ought not to continue in the ranks of the ministry, and the probabilities are against their being successful in a business which is recognized to be close and hazardous. The place of a Book Agent should not be filled by men past middle life or played-out men; when a minister becomes an expert book publisher, he has lost his adaptation to the travelling ministry. Secular and money questions will occupy his time so thoroughly that preparation for ministerial service will be interfered with. Why is it that ministers who have held official positions in the church, places that are largely secular in their working, so rarely re-enter the active work of the ministry? Why is it that ministerial agents of church boards generally meet empty houses? The reader can answer.

RELIGIOUS NEWSPAPERS.

The policy of the church as to the number and character of the religious newspapers published under its authority merits careful consideration. The newspapers are the popular teachers, distributors of general knowledge, recorders of current history, and express public opinion.

They furnish a running commentary on the doings of the world; they are indispensable to an active and vigorous church; they promulgate and defend its teachings and usages; through them the members should be free to communicate their well-digested thoughts as to its every interest; they furnish the pabulum on which many families acquire all their knowledge of Christian work and of the world's life; they do much to promote the unity of the church; their influence for good is probably greater in proportion to cost than any other outside work of the church.

The providing such a means of influence is, then, one of the most important duties of the Methodist Episcopal Church. How this can be done, within the province of a church, is the question that it is proposed now to discuss.

The adopted policy of the Methodist Episcopal Church, for more than a half-century, has been to provide its members with religious newspapers. This policy was based on a recognition of the same principle which led the church to establish the Book Concerns,—viz., its duty to provide proper instruction and reading for the people. The result has been that there are now ten weekly religious newspapers published under its control.

While it is conceded that it is the duty of the church to take care that its people may have proper religious books to read; and that with a church so widely extended and so intimately connected in interest as ours, it should have one or two newspapers of the highest character; yet, whether the adopted policy of the church, of furnishing the members with all their religious newspapers, is wise, is quite another question. If this policy is to be continued, then, as the membership of the church increases in all directions, at home and abroad, there must come, in time, a large increase in their number. The different sections of this country must be supplied, as well as the members in foreign lands.* If such addition to their number is to be in the ratio of the present Conference papers, in place of ten there will be twenty, thirty, or forty. An accompanying result of this would be the issue of a flood of inferior local papers to supply home news. This tendency is now apparent, and will increase as local interests may require.

The counter-policies that may be suggested are to leave the publication of religious newspapers exclusively to private enterprise, as is done by the other

---

* The action of the recent Conferences in India shows how strongly the tendency and desire are to have the news- and other published papers for their local uses and interests.

denominations, or that the church should control one or two papers, leaving to private enterprise the furnishing of papers for local circulation.

The reasons favoring the first plan of supplying all the wants of the church in religious newspapers, are, that by it the church secures a supply of reading for its members; that the church determines the character of the teaching, forms the opinions of its members, and furnishes the papers at a low price. The first and last reasons, while partially true, yet are met by the fact that there is now no difficulty in securing publishers of newspapers under Methodist patronage, if they can have a fair field, and are not handicapped by the official press. There is sufficient private enterprise to meet all the wants of the members at a fair price. When anything is given to the people under cost it must be as a charity, a mission work, or with the expectation of future profit; if the church publishes papers at a loss for the use of a people who can afford to pay a fair price, then it is a waste of money contributed for other purposes. Such publication at a loss may be proper for purely mission work, but the loss should be charged to the missionary treasury. The expectation of future profit may be a good business reason, if not carried too far. But, as to the second reason, which influences the present policy of the church, there is more ground for question. That the character of the religious teaching of the newspapers read by our people should be conserved by the oversight of the church seems almost an axiom; yet, owing to the fact that the publication of so many papers prevents the establishment of others, of equal or higher character, by private enterprise, the result is produced that the sole control of the religious newspapers of the Methodist Episcopal Church is in the ministry, through the election of the editors by the General Conference.

Out of the seeming axiom just named there spring the important questions, Whether the entire church press should be under the control of the ministry? Should the ministers have the exclusive power of forming the opinions of the church? Should they have the power, through their control of the press, of preventing the full and free discussion of any question connected with the interests of Methodism? Do they not by this power have in their grasp its usefulness; indeed, its life? Does not this fact of the acknowledged power of the ministry give the editors of the church papers an influence in the church that they should not have? Is it not the record of history that whenever such power has existed it has inevitably led to its abuse? Are not rings, as they are vulgarly called, the immediate result of such united influence and power? Are not the unholy ambitions of men excited under such conditions? Are not such editors in danger of yielding to the force of temptation and becoming so demoralized that the end thereof is disgrace to themselves and injury to the church? If a favorable answer cannot be given to these queries, what can be hoped for, with the future extension of the church and its system of church papers, scattered all over a vaunted œcumenical Methodism?

What will be the character of the members of the

Methodist Episcopal Church who will continue to be willing to have their mouths thus shut upon all questions of church government or policy, or what kind of ministers will the church have, who dare not express a thought contrary to that of the ring that may control the press? How does a muzzled press harmonize with the teaching of republicanism, that a free press must exist in a free country? Absolute governments control: free governments encourage the press. The world gains in wisdom by the variety of thoughts and suggestions made in free discussion. There is no advance in thought through a muzzled press. A muzzled press narrows its readers in mind, thought, experience, and influence; a free press enlarges the mind, broadens the thought, deepens the experience, of its readers. The church is and must be the loser by the absence of free discussion. All these objections exist to-day as to the church newspapers.

There is another view of this question of the control of the teachings of the press. The apparent axiomatic truth alluded to is the basis on which the Church of Rome has been built. It squarely assumes the right to say what books shall be read by its people, what their literature shall be; the Bible, if read at all, must be read as printed by its translation of the early manuscripts. But it does not assume to directly control the religious newspapers; they are left free. Neither the English Church in England, nor the Presbyterian Churches in the United States, nor any evangelical denomination assumes to furnish its people with the religious newspaper. While the ministers of the Methodist Episcopal Church, like their brethren in the Catholic priesthood, control the organization of their church, its real estate (except in certain States), and its purse, yet they have a power, beyond the ambition of the Pope at Rome, in their absolute control of the church press, by furnishing not only the literature, but the very newspapers their members shall read.

Ministers well understand the power of the religious press in fostering inquiries, creating thought, and forming opinion, as well as the narrowing and unhealthy influence of the presentation of one side only of a question, of creating prejudice against existing church laws, or favor for proposed changes, of a failure to tell the whole truth, or of the many evils that accompany the exclusive power to reach and influence a confiding people through the papers they read. Is it not, then, clear that the continuation of the present policy will increase the danger to the church from the ministry as a body,—by the increase of elective officers; by the influence of increased amount of capital employed; by the tendencies of such increase of official places to create rings, centralize influence, and concentrate power; by unwise legislation through control of minds uneducated by free discussion, and by the dissatisfaction that will be felt by many of the ministry and laity?

If, then, this description of the results of the continuation of the present policy of the church as to its religious papers is correct, it becomes an important inquiry to know what should be done to escape these dangers.

The other two suggestions must then be examined: First: That the supply of such papers should be left free, or that no papers should be published by the church. Second: That the church should publish one or more papers for general circulation, leaving to private enterprise to supply local necessities. These propositions may be considered together. The wisdom of the church, in securing to the membership through the religious newspaper a general knowledge of its passing history, of what is being done in the various fields of church work, cannot be questioned. Nor is the wisdom to be doubted of having a certain medium of bringing before the members the demands of Christ's cause, as they open to the church; a medium for the defence of the church, a fitting place for discussion of all questions of morals and religion, and, properly, all questions of polity; of keeping a record of the saints that are passing away; and of doing all the work that is accepted as the proper duty of such papers. One properly-prepared paper would supply the demands just noted and meet the wants of the church, and with this provision its duty ends. The further wants of the members should be left to private enterprise. There would then be established as needed independent newspapers of a suitable character to meet local wants. Such papers would maintain a higher rank than the present Conference papers, and it would give an opening for one or more of the highest character. Such papers would be untrammelled by the presence of local church papers under ministerial control, and a free discussion of church policy and interests would be possible. The presence of such a press would force proper treatment of all contributors by the authorized church paper, and secure in it a free expression of opinion. Under the present policy all the efforts to establish independent Methodist newspapers have failed, with the exception of the *Zion's Herald,* which has had a vigorous life for many years, due to causes that are not necessary to name.

The Methodist, to which the laity of the church owe the introduction of lay representation in the General Conference in 1872, could not be sustained after the realization of its great work. It was felt as a conservative power, and exerted a strong influence in preventing unwise changes in the discipline and polity of the church. The control of the church press was changed by the General Conference of 1876, through its influence on the mind of the church. The principal church paper was forced to raise its literary standard to meet that of its competitor.

The Methodist, an honor to its founders, did a grand work for the church; yet it could not be sustained against the influence of the church papers, the church rings, the Book-Room influences, and the hostility of a party in the ministry. The possibility of a repetition of such influence can only be prevented, first, by the removal of such power, and next, by the encouragement of an independent press.

By such a policy our members would be better served by having one first-class paper, which should exceed in value any religious newspaper now published. It would have behind it a membership of over two millions, and, if properly conducted, could be profitably sold at such low figures as to insure a very large circulation. Increase in quality brings decrease in price. To secure such a paper, there must be liberality on the part of the publishers and fitting ability in the editor. He must not be the principal writer and strain his mind to produce variety. His business should be to edit the papers of other writers.

The editors of the church press have very generally fallen into the grave error of making the papers too personal as to themselves. In newspapers published by private individuals there need be no limit; it is a question between them and their readers. But a paper published by a church for the education and edification of its members should not be used for the glorification of its editor, or as the medium of communicating his views on any and all subjects. The ablest editors rarely contribute to their own papers, and they leave no marks in their writings to identify them; individuality is buried. The influence of the paper depends on the ability of its editorials, its communications, and correspondence. This personal character of the Methodist Church press has had a tendency to lower the respect for the editors, for the press, and for the church; it has always been in bad taste and has displayed an unfortunate ignorance of the proprieties of the place, and the object and duties for which an editor was chosen. Again, there is no need that an editor of a religious paper should be a preacher. Dr. Bond, a layman, had a better style of editorial writing than any editor of the Advocate, before or since his time. In fact, ministers as a class are not the best writers for the press; their style partakes too much of the volubility of the pulpit; the same objection holds good as to orators and ready speech-makers. A certain condensation in language, accuracy in use of words and crispness of thought, are requisite to the successful newspaper writer; of these few men are the masters. The editorials of Dr. Bond, of Horace Greeley, and of Dr. Crooks illustrate this idea. The church will be the gainer by thus relieving the active ministry from any demand for their services as editors.

The church would thus secure a local press that would be suited to the wants of each district of country, and in literary character be in advance of the present average of Conference papers. This would be aided by the dependence of the owners of such a press on their own efforts for success; they would have no treasury of a rich church behind them. The church would be saved from the increasing number of very inferior local papers that are springing up in the Conferences under the present policy; they cost many times more than a good paper in proportion to value, and this cost prevents many of their subscribers from taking in addition the better papers of the church. This evil of local papers is growing so rapidly that the last General Conference practically re-enacted the following resolution: "That the Annual Conferences are affectionately and earnestly requested not to establish any more Conference papers, and when such papers exist, to discontinue them when it can be done consistently with existing obligations." (Discipline, 1884, p. 351.) This plan for furnishing our members with religious newspapers would give fair play to discussion and to the expression of their multitudinous opinions that would relieve the church as the thunder-storm relieves the atmosphere of pressure. It would educate the membership in all directions, and would fully meet the wants of the church. There need be no fear of the results of such freedom of the press. The church is too strongly planted in the hearts of the laity to permit evil to come to it through their support of independent papers.

That no organized body in the church should be authorized to publish newspapers, except under the direct authority and control of the General Conference, needs no proof.

Taking all things into consideration, it is a safe inference that the safety and prosperity of the church, both largely involved in the decision of this question, would be secured and promoted by a change of the policy of the publication of newspapers as recommended. Finally, the same objection lies to the election of editors by the General Conference as to that of Book Agents, and enforces the argument that such selection should be made by the Book Committee. It is practically out of the question to depend on the multitude of a General Conference to make a good selection of so important an official and one requiring such peculiar qualifications.

QUARTERLY REVIEW.

A church properly equipped for the education of its ministers and members requires, in addition to a provision for the elaborate discussion of religious questions in the book and the provision of a weekly press, a periodical of the style and character of the leading reviews of this country and Europe. It should be of the highest scholastic and literary character, that the church may contribute its share to the investigations and learning of the world. A part of the work of such a review should be to note and discuss the advancement of science, the developments of the buried past, the researches and discoveries of the learned, the results of the investigations into the original texts of the word of God, the collateral arguments these afford to enforce the truths of the Bible, and the preparation of the people for the coming of Jesus Christ; the elucidation of many of his teachings which in the past were uncertain in their meaning, making the clearer understanding and the acceptation of the doctrine both possible and practical. It should be a part of its work also to note, discuss, and expose the errors taught by many professing and non-professing Christians; to keep its readers in connection with the learning of the day; and, above all, to be a defender of Christianity and its civilization. Such a periodical would offer a fitting home for the scholarly work of our teachers and students. It is necessary as a defence of our church polity and faith. The defence of the faith of a church depends on the learning as well as on the piety of its teachers. The establishment of such a "Review" would be an evidence that the Methodist Episcopal Church is willing to recognize and perform all its duties.

If there are not in the church a sufficient number of writers to sustain such a Review with their own productions, then there is the greater need that other writers should be employed to educate the Methodist clergy and people in the higher branches of theological literature. These remarks are suggested by the unfortunate action of the recent General Conference in not providing for this want of the church.

The passing out of the former editor, who, after his years of earnest work, sought rest, was a fitting opportunity to replace the *Quarterly Review* on the level it held in 1856, under the editorship of the Rev. Dr. John McClintock.

It may be that the ministerial delegates of the General Conference of 1884 had some remembrance of the action of the Indianapolis Conference of 1856, when it declined to re-elect that distinguished minister of God to the editorship of the *Quarterly Review* because its literary character was too high and its articles were too learned for the average minister. The result was attained with an annual deficit in the revenues and the desired lower standard of the *Review*. But with the lapse of twenty-eight years, and the higher education of the ministry, it could have reasonably been expected that the General Conference would make a point of the selection of some younger man who was fully competent, and had in all probability several years of good work before him, to take charge of the *Review* and restore it to its lost position of a learned and influential journal. If this had been done there would have been no trouble as to its circulation, nor any deficiency in cost. It is folly to expect that educated men and earnest students will be willing to accept very common fare when so many richly-spread tables are offered them by other churches. The General Conference failed to appreciate the interests of the ministry, and of the church at large, by not making proper provision for their representative magazine, the *Quarterly Review*.*

So much for the practical side of this question of the publishing interests.

There is another yet more important consideration which will influence the church in deciding upon the policy of continuing the Book Concerns, viz., the danger to the church from the gathering together of so many official representatives in one building and in one city. Man is a gregarious animal, and officials are men, and are tempted to unite and help each other to retain their places. To do this involves the temptation to combine to govern the church. Of such combinations the Book-Rooms in the past have been the centre. The use of the credit of the church by an agent in New York; the stealings and demoralization of employès; the unholy attempt to crush a man as honest as steel, and as firm in the right as the everlasting rocks, because he dared expose such use and such frauds, developed the power of such a combination of officials with their parasites. It showed the danger to the church of the control of these interests

---

* Since the above was written the further lowering of the standard of the *Quarterly Review* has been consummated, and the Methodist Episcopal Church, with its ministry, its membership, its universities, colleges, theological schools, etc., is left without a representative magazine in the higher circle of theological and learned utterances.

by the ministers, and the questionable prudence or wisdom of permitting, unless under the highest necessity, such an amount of property and such a large capital in money to accumulate in any one place.

It is acknowledged, with pleasure, that there have been in recent years great advances made in the management of the Book Concern in New York. The clear-minded Nelson with his business habits commenced changes in its policy which have been vigorously followed up by Mr. Phillips, and this branch of the Book Concern is undoubtedly doing better work and at lower prices and on surer business principles than ever before. This result of the work of these two laymen (for Dr. Nelson was practically a layman) is a proof of the position taken in these pages, that the management of the Book Concerns should be under the control of laymen educated to the business: the policy regulating the scope of the business is another matter.

Further, it is highly creditable to the agents of both Concerns that for the last twelve years no shadow of suspicion as to their integrity has been thrown on any of them, but this is no argument or security for the future. There is in the very nature of such institutions a temptation to those who are in office to retain their places; to many who are out to get possession of them; and to the ambitious, to gain the control of them as a means of securing greater power and higher positions in the church. Of the force of this latter temptation the history of the church is full of examples, and as these publishing interests develop with the growth of the country and the additions to the membership, so will the temptation to make a bad use of official places increase. The Church of Christ was never intended to be degraded to a money-making machine, or to be used as a means of putting men up or down. For all such misuse a fitting penalty will be incurred.

The last General Conference, by formal change of Discipline, adopted the argument of this paper by providing that the editors of the Reviews and newspapers published by the Book Agents may be "either ministers or members of the Methodist Episcopal Church" (Discipline, page 339). The same rule as to Book Agents has been in operation for some years. This action of the General Conference is important, as it reveals the facts:

First: That in the judgment of the Conference there are men in both orders, clerical and lay, competent to fill such places.

Secondly: That it does not require the use of ministerial education or functions to properly perform the duties of such places.

Thirdly: It is a fair inference from the above that when a minister, called of God to preach His gospel, performs the duties of an editor he is acting as a layman.

Fourthly: That when an effective itinerant minister accepts such a place, for whatever good reason, and such may exist, he should be placed in a suspended list or take rank as a local preacher.

The same arguments apply to Book Agents. These statements, expositions, and suggestions as to the general benevolent and publishing work of the church reveal, if nothing more, the necessity that exists for a thorough revision of the policy of the church in respect thereto. To make the best use of these powers for good will require a reconstruction of their management, of their scope of work, and, to a great extent, of the principles on which most of them are now based and managed.

CHAPTER IV.

The injury that will result to the church from temptations to which the ministry are subjected, which while personal, yet have an influence on the church, and also from the tendency to form alliances for securing influence and control for their benefit as a class, or party.

FIRST: THE MINISTRY AS A CLASS.

A VERY potent argument in favor of the introduction of lay representatives into all the councils, boards, and business of the Methodist Episcopal Church is to be found in the dangers that may come from the combined action of the ministry as a class. The history of the world is full of the errors and wrongs committed against the people by Pagan and Roman priests and the ministers of the Protestant Churches. In no single instance have they had the supremacy for a long time without abusing it. It began within a few years after the death of the Apostles, and has continued until this day. In the churches, other than the papal and the Methodist Episcopal, the people have secured protection, by having the control of the church equally divided between the laity and the clergy. This division of authority has in all instances, when fairly conducted, resulted to the benefit of both parties.

The dangers to be apprehended by the continuance

of the control of the ministry over the Methodist Episcopal Church are those exemplified in the history of the Roman Catholic Church, in the earliest English Church, and so far as such power has been exercised, in other churches. How it works will be seen by some examples of the temptations to which the ministers of the Methodist Episcopal Church are peculiarly liable.

SECOND: POLITICAL TEMPTATIONS AND LOSS OF AGGRESSIVENESS.

In an early part of this paper allusion was made to the dangers to the usefulness of the church as a body, arising from the temptation to engage in political partisanship and from decreased aggressiveness. It may be well to notice more particularly the injurious influence these temptations have on the ministry.

The extent of the first danger will be readily comprehended by any one who has observed how readily the ministers of the different denominations are led into political and semi-political controversies. This is a result of the assumed influence of the ministers over the members of the churches. The Methodist ministers being supposed to understand the masses of the people and to have most direct access to and influence over them, their opinions are used very freely by politicians. Designing politicians of the baser sort, who strive to work up for selfish purposes some new party on moral grounds, make a direct effort to secure Methodist ministers as their agents, because on all moral and religious questions the clergy are regarded as leaders of the people. The strength of this temptation is found in the ease with which ministers abandon their proper duties, and become partisan temperance and moral reform lecturers, political speech makers, office-holders, etc.

It bodes no good to the church when its ministry, or any considerable proportion of it, are smitten with the love of political influence, are flattered by men, who first use and then despise them, for their lack of fidelity to their calling. This is no thoughtless suggestion of danger, because the efforts that are constantly being made to use their influence for party purposes are well understood. They form a well-known element in political calculations, and the church is scarcely aware how many yield to the temptation.

As the church is made up of individual members, any peril that threatens the whole body from without will reach each member; and any danger that threatens the whole body from its inner life will first be felt by the individual members. Dangers from without can be more readily met than those that have their rise in the members of the body. The danger of being enticed into political strife owes its strength to the ambition of the individual members; the danger from the loss of an aggressive spirit has its origin in the decay of spiritual life in the ministry and membership. The temptations that come in this line to the ministers are insidious; they come with success and with public favor. Worldly influences gathering around them, they do not feel so deeply that the gospel, committed to their charge, is intended for the poor in this world's goods. A comfortable church, a well-to-do people, and a fair support are more pleasant and attractive than a mission to the poor. The fact that this is a natural preference includes the danger that is in it. Jesus Christ, in sending forth his disciples, did not wish them to follow their natural preferences, but the reverse; the law to them was to go wherever man was to be found and to preach the gospel to him. The church will have to protect its ministry against the influence of these temptations.

THIRD: UNACCEPTABLE MINISTERS.

The third danger arises from the efforts of ministers who have lost their usefulness to retain their official connection with the Annual Conferences. The temptation comes to them through the value of their claim to an appointment; that is, for their support and the financial aid they may be entitled to as members of aid societies, or recipients of the moneys contributed for the help of the worthy. Such men are in the way of other ministers and are an incubus on the church; they lower it in public estimation and stand in the way of its progress.

To retain the ministry in the regular work, with a scant and uncertain support, was one of the difficulties of the church in its early days, and, as a consequence, many were forced to locate. That this difficulty no longer exists is a cause for thankfulness. The provision of the law of the church which gives to every minister, in good standing, an appointment, secures to him a better average support, taking all things into consideration, than is received by the ministers of any other church.

This certain support has been given as one reason why it is so hard to get rid of many men in the Conferences who have outlived their usefulness. It needs no argument to show how degrading it is to the manhood and Christian character of a preacher who holds to his place in the Conference for its money, when he knows that he is no longer acceptable to the people, and that his usefulness as a minister has ceased. They, too, often forget that the church was not intended for an indolent man's refuge, or as an eleemosynary institution, nor a home for men who fail to perform the work the church expected and that they agreed to do when they were admitted to its ministry. The contract between the church and the minister which secured the latter a place to work in, a support while working, and some aid in his declining years, is broken when the minister ceases through his own fault to do the full service of a preacher of the gospel of Jesus Christ.

If the law of the church could be made so searching that every member of a Conference who was not actively and successfully engaged in the service of the church should lose his membership, be located or dropped from the ministry, it would do much to relieve many of them from their false position. The older Conferences are loaded down with unacceptable men. They claim all the rights and powers of the active and useful men: the right to take part in the deliberations of the Annual Conferences; the right to vote; to be elected to the General Conference; to share in the contributions made for the relief of the worthy, and to be counted in the number which gives a General Conference representative; and when other means of support fail, to ask, if supernumeraries, to be restored to the active list.

In this class of the ministry are to be found the jealous, the discontented, and the conceited. They are the principal complainants against the bishops and presiding elders for the character of their appointments. They find fault with the church government, because it involves in the performance of their duties some self-denial and some religious experience. Their work is formally done, without life or interest. The collection of their stipend is the one thing they faithfully look after. These men favor the extension of the time of service. They object to running the gauntlet of acceptability every two or three years. This class of the ministry are an injury to the church, and their presence in an Annual Conference is an injustice to the active ministers. The Conferences need a thorough cleaning out of such thistles: they choke the growing grain.

How to get rid of these men has been and is yet a problem. General Conferences have struggled with it without much success; their plans have been thwarted by the members of the Annual Conferences. The suggestion hereinbefore made, that all membership in an Annual Conference should be confined to certain classes of the ministry, who are accepted as being properly employed in the teaching, preaching, and pastoral service of the church, and in the care of its benevolent interests, would meet this case of unacceptable ministers. In this way they might retain their membership in the ministry or could become local preachers.

FOURTH: SECULARIZATION OF THE MINISTRY.

A fourth danger to the ministers arises from the force of the temptation to abandon their proper work for official positions and secular employment.

As the Methodist Episcopal Church increased in numbers, intelligence, and wealth, God gave it a position of corresponding influence, and opened to it various fields of labor in the way of missionary and benevolent work, church building, educating its people in academies, colleges, and theological schools; in teaching the young the Bible; in providing religious newspapers, tracts, and in the preparation and publication of proper magazines and books. To do the work in this widely-extended field, the ministers were at hand, with seemingly the best-suited talents and acquirements for such work, and their services could be obtained at the lowest price. Very naturally the secretaries, professors, editors, and publishers were chosen from that body; indeed, there was a necessity for their temporary use. This use, this filling such offices from the ministry, has gone on during the years without question, until now the holding of these places has acquired an almost universal acceptance in the minds of the ministers as in some way their peculiar right. As such positions were originally filled by accomplished and able men, they naturally gained great influence in the church's councils; they were respected, trusted, and beloved by the membership. But like many other customs that have grown out of the necessities of the case, this fitness has created a desire for official positions, which has reached a point where it has become an undue temptation to very many of the ministry to leave their proper work for almost any semi-religious or secular employment. For some years past the seemingly greatest source of interest in the meeting of a General Conference has not been what could be done to advance through the church the cause of the Master, but who should fill the offices. Or if this expression be too strong, the anxiety upon the point has divided the attention of the Conference with more important subjects. As the holders of General Conference positions have generally been selected by the Annual Conferences as delegates to the General Conference, and, as the ambitious and leading men of the Annual Conferences are usually also delegates, it is evident that among the members of the General Conference there will be found few ministers who are not in some way hopeful of, or that stand a chance of, being selected for some one of the official or honorary positions. In the General Conference of 1884, two hundred and ten of the two hundred and sixty-five ministerial delegates received votes for some official position, and three hundred and seventy names were used for the one hundred and eighty-six official positions and honorary appointments. It is also a notable fact that it rarely occurs that any one is elected for a General Conference position who is not a member of that body. It does not require much thought to comprehend wherein or how such a desire for place, with its attendant electioneering, is injurious to the ministry.

Some of the suggested recommendations would work very beneficially in the way of reducing this evil, by transferring the power of selecting the secretaries, editors, and Book Agents to their respective boards and committees, and by introducing such safeguards as would render the choice of a bishop by unwise and improper means exceedingly difficult, if not impossible. But there is a more serious view. The time is rapidly coming, if not now, when the church will more carefully investigate the propriety and the results of this holding of places by its preachers, and will ask why the pulpit and the pastorate should be deprived of the services of men to do work that could be as well done by laymen or local preachers. The church will ask, How can a minister, called of God to preach His gospel, accept the office of editor, publisher, or an agency of any kind, always excepting the leading Bible societies, while he has the health and strength to do the work of a pastor, is acceptable to some church, and is sure of a reasonable support, and when there is no pressing church necessity for his leaving the proper work of a Christian minister? It is at this point where the temptation comes in to cause the chosen ones—the called of God—to lower their colors, forsake their high calling, and follow the dictates of ambition, of love of power, of influence, or of bodily comfort. It is easy to broaden out God's command to preach His gospel so as to include all these offices, and very many others, as part of their work. Many commands of Jesus

Christ are made elastic enough, by the ingenuity of man, to cover more surface than was intended. There is danger to the ministry in this looseness of construction and disposition to make Christ's call suit their preferences.

When once the proper line of duty is left, no matter by how small a divergence, the way is opened to stretch it that it may cover the ordinary duties of a member of the church, and yet to claim that ministerial work is done, because, in some indirect and irregular way, the man may be preaching the gospel. If any effective minister can do as good work in the petty offices of tract agencies, book publishing, editing newspapers, etc., as he could in the regular work, then such fact is sufficient evidence why he should retire from the travelling ministry. The law of the church should be enforced at this point, and be reaffirmed by the provisions already suggested as to terms of membership in an Annual Conference. The anomalous position of many preachers in claiming to hold one place by the power of a certain call from God while performing the duties of another should not be permitted. It is a wrong to the church, to the laity, and to the active ministry.

A further discussion of the meaning of "the call from God to preach the gospel," including its character and extent, may help to put this question of holding church and secular offices in a clearer light. While a call to preach is fully accepted as placing on a man the performance of a certain duty, yet it is fair to recognize the fact that this call may be for a peculiar work and for a certain time; that it may be withdrawn or suspended, not necessarily from any want of fitness for continued service in preaching the gospel, or from unfaithfulness, but it may come from greater fitness for other work, through increased knowledge and greater wisdom; or it may be affected by age, loss of health, of voice, or many other like and good reasons. A call to preach is not necessarily permanent and continuous through life. The point desired to be made is, that when other work than teaching and preaching is to be done, even though it be in the Master's vineyard, and teaching and preaching are suspended, then such ministers should promptly rearrange their relation to the church to suit their new work. Such a change is consistent with the suspension or the withdrawal of "a call to preach."

An analysis of the duties of some of the officials of the church will prove how incongruous they are with the work of the ministry, and will be the best defence of the proposition that their relations to the church should be changed. Take the case of an editor of a church newspaper. Is editing a religious newspaper preaching the gospel? In any proper sense, is the preaching done in the paper, by the editorials, by religious essays, by extracts from old sermons, by witty puns and amusing stories, as effective as proper work in the pulpit? Does the paper make pastoral visits as often and just when needed? Does it convince the impenitent, lead him to Christ, watch and aid him in his struggles to cut loose from the dominion of Satan? Does it point him to the simplicity of faith in Christ, and tenderly care for him in his early experience? Does it visit the sick-bed, pray over the dying father, mother, wife, or child? Does it offer the consolation which is reasonably expected of a sympathizing pastor? Does it bury the dead? In fine, is the editor of a paper performing the proper duties of a travelling minister in the Methodist Episcopal Church? Certainly not. That he does no work which cannot be as well done by a layman is practically confessed by the *Christian Advocate* of December 4, 1884, wherein it is published " that the *principal* business of the *Christian Advocate*, as stated in the prospectus, is to explain, illustrate, confirm, and, if necessary, defend Methodism." This certainly is not preaching the gospel. The ability to defend the Methodist Church, or to explain, illustrate, and confirm her teachings and customs, is not confined to the ministry.

What position does a Book Agent hold? Is the publication of all kinds of books that will pay a profit the work of a travelling minister? Is he preaching the everlasting truths of Christ's gospel to dying men when he issues a history, a dictionary, or a work of fiction? Is the mixing in the affairs of the world, coming in business competition with men of the church and men of the world, studying the changes in the market-prices of stuffs, preaching the gospel of Christ? Is he filling the place of a pastor in the church? Is he subject to the trials of the itinerancy? Does he have the benefit of its joys and successes? Does his labor in getting a book on the market and making money out of it convince any one of sin and the judgment to come? Is he doing the great and noble work of an effective travelling Methodist minister? Certainly not.

In these suggestive queries it must be borne in mind that the objection is not to the men who now hold or have held these positions; they have merely followed the usages of the church; nor to the work, nor to the policy, of the church in the past or at this date; but we are looking to the future, to the danger there is to the ministry in this temptation to obtain and hold secular and semi-religious offices in the church. Our object is to show the incongruity of such relations, and the defect of the organization of the church at this point.

This argument for limiting the ministry to their proper work is more forcible in the Methodist Episcopal Church than in any other religious organization, because every effective preacher has his appointed ministerial duties. He is not dependent for his support on securing secular employment. When he accepts an office which is not strictly within his call, he gives up the work to which he has asserted, before God and man, that he felt "inwardly moved by the Holy Ghost" to do.

Another reason may be named. The fact that the men selected for the official positions are generally men of mark in the church is an argument why they should be kept in the pastorate. If they are highly educated; if they have natural gifts and acquired powers of oratory; if they are leaders of men, then the pastorate offers the best use for such gifts. It secures for them, through its itinerancy, the widest influence. It is making the best use of the ability God has bestowed upon them

Such men are not so numerous that they can be spared for inferior and secular work. On the other side, the executive offices of the church require a superior grade of men to make them successful, and are not fit places for even able ministers in their declining years; they all require the energy and hopefulness of early manhood. The only safe rule, then, that the church can adopt in selecting men for the various offices of the church is to limit the use of effective travelling preachers to offices that require the use of ministerial functions.

The same law should apply to the inferior offices in the Annual Conferences, and to appointments to charitable and local societies.

From this exposition of one of the principal temptations of Methodist preachers it may be profitable to establish the proper religious attitude of a minister towards church offices. If the ambition of a man is to acquire office simply for its emoluments, honor, or ease, then such ambition is based on pure selfishness; if he feels an inward consciousness of ability to creditably perform its duties, the grade of selfishness is lessened; but if a man couples with such conscious ability a strong desire to better the condition of his fellow-men or to increase the usefulness of the church; if it is his conviction that he can do more for Christ's cause by holding office, then such ambition may be honorable. These grades of ambition for the offices of government or of society may be pardonable, and even honorable, but when the question of suitability to fill responsible positions in the church is brought face to face with human ambition, the really good man, even though believing himself to be the best for the place, will shrink from pressing his own suit, and will trust to the sense of his fitness being first discovered and suggested by his brethren. The invocation of divine guidance in a selection may then be a solemn act, and not an insult and a sacrilege, as it is when the selection has been previously made and agreed upon by a caucus, or by friends, and the form of supplication is used as a cloak.

While it is acknowledged with thankfulness that there are ministers in official position in the Methodist Episcopal Church who are comprised in the latter class, yet it must be acknowledged with deep sorrow and mortification that, judging impartially from all attainable facts, there have been some who were not.

There is also a constant temptation to several classes of ministers to get into all the little places connected with the Annual Conferences, to edit local newspapers, holiness journals, to buy and sell books, and to represent benevolent associations in the cities and towns. The applicants for these positions form a second series in the line of office-seekers. The first series, already described, seek General Conference places; this second series are willing to take a range of places with less pay, less honor, and probably more ease. They are often men who have been touched with the desire of money-making, are speculators in camp-meeting and seaside town lots, and use the religion of Christ as an element in making money. Many of the applicants for these places are men who feel they have been neglected, that their talents have not been appreciated, that they are worthy of better than small appointments, and that the church has not been willing to take them at their own valuation; they are men whose zeal has cooled; who have become lazy and unacceptable; who are unwilling to acknowledge that their call to preach has been withdrawn, and sever honorably their connection with a Conference. They hold on for the chances of getting, through their ministerial relation, some other employment than that of their Master. There is very often, in these petty offices, a temptation to the younger men, in their hours of exhaustion and depression, to wish for lighter work.

But there is a class of men, in connection with the Annual Conferences, who may desire such places without an imputation on their motives or Christian character; men who have served the church faithfully, and yet may feel that a time has come when, for various good reasons, their active services in the ministry should cease.

Every effort should be made to save our ministers from what seems to be an universal temptation to men of that order in all countries and in all Protestant Churches,—viz., To get out of the regular work of the ministry and to engage in employments that are, in their essence, secular. This tendency to the secularization of the ministry must be stopped, or the cause of Christ will suffer.

FIFTH: METHODS OF SECURING POWER THROUGH ALLIANCES OF THE MINISTRY AS A CLASS.

The fifth temptation of the ministry is to be found in the attempt to secure, by concert of action as a class, certain changes in the organization of the church.

In the following criticisms on this evil it is proper to write that, while the motives of men cannot be read and should not be impugned, yet it is fair to trace effects back to their causes, and leave the labor of harmonizing them with wisdom, prudence, and religion to those who originate the means that produce the results. Combination does not necessarily involve consultation; when two or more men work in the same line, use the same tools, and the operations of each are known to the other, the effect is the same as though done after consultation. This effort to secure a concert of action to build up a ministerial hierarchy has been for some years steadily pursued; men now hoary-headed have been sowing the seeds of distrust among the preachers, and urging upon them the necessity of united action for self-protection. The movement has proven attractive to some of the younger and more ambitious men; they are dazzled with its promised honors, place, and influence; they have not had sufficient experience in life to see its results. Whether the efforts in this line had their origin in disappointed ambition, the failure of hopes, the inability to secure some high office, a failure to comprehend the breadth and mission of Methodism, or whatever may have been the cause, it is impossible to say. Yet so it is; work in this direction has been going on for a number of years.

To exclude the laity from any further representation in the councils of the church is the *first* verse of this

New Testament; to attack the bishops' power and to place a limit on the length of their service is the *second;* to build up the Annual Conference as a recognized power with certain legislative and administrative rights is the *third.* The last two points of attack are divisible into three:

First: To elect the bishops at each General Conference for a four years' term, to lessen their influence in the church by disregarding and underrating their advice, and to take from them the sole power of appointment.

Second: By changing the law of the church as to term of service.

Third: By increasing the power and influence of the Annual Conference.

If they can succeed in excluding the laity from any further representation, in controlling the appointments, in lengthening the time of service, and strengthening the Annual Conference, they will have retaken the citadel of the church just at the time it has been thought their control was disappearing.

BY EXCLUSION OF LAITY FROM CHURCH COUNCILS.

If these charges are true the danger is imminent, and our members should awake to their importance. The careful observers of the passing history of the church will note the following, among other facts that might be produced, and make their own inferences: That a majority of the ministry were opposed to the introduction of lay representation into the General Conferences in 1868 and 1872, that they yielded it under pressure, and that a majority of them are to-day opposed to any further introduction of the laity, either into the General or Annual Conferences, or to a reconstruction of the Quarterly Conference. The defeat of the efforts made in the General Conferences of 1880 and 1884 to increase lay representation in the General Conference and to introduce it into the Annual Conferences tells its own story. The appointment of a committee on lay representation by the last General Conference, in place of favorable action, was an act unworthy of that body. This action of the ministry (the lords of Methodism) was on a par with that of the House of Lords in England on the franchise bill: one wanted a report on lay representation in 1888, the other a redistribution bill in advance of the passage of the franchise bill. Both wanted to throttle the movement, as they were based on the same principle,—the one to enfranchise the two million members of the Methodist Episcopal Church, the other to enfranchise two millions of the laborers of England. This class tendency will continue to defeat all efforts for change until the laity arise and demand their rights as Christian men and women to a full and equal share in the work of the Church of Jesus Christ. The membership should never lose sight of the fact that classes of men are persistent in retaining power; they quickly discover when its possession is threatened, and readily combine for mutual protection and defence.

BY ATTACK ON THE POWER AND INFLUENCE OF THE BISHOPS.

Before considering the attack on the bishops it may be well to examine their relation to the organization of the church, and the power they have in its administration.

BISHOPS, THEIR RELATION TO AND POWER IN THE CHURCH.

The bishops are elected for life, with the right of resignation. Their duties are almost exclusively administrative. They preside at all sessions of the General and Annual Conferences, in which sessions they have no vote, and are not admitted to the privileges of the floor. From their decision in the General Conference there is the right of appeal to the body itself. Their decisions in the Annual Conference can only be reversed through an appeal to the General Conference. They have, therefore, no absolute power of decision; further, it is their duty to appoint the ministers as they find them on the rolls of each Conference, the members of the Conference determining who are the ministers to be appointed. This appointing power is absolute. The character of the bishops, the amount of work done in the previous four years, and their methods of performing their work, are examined by a committee at each General Conference. In the meetings of the joint committees of the Missionary and Church Extension Boards, each bishop is entitled to one vote. If it were provided in the reconstruction of the boards and societies that all committees should consist of an equal number of clerical and lay representatives, there would be no objection to this right of voting, as it is the only instance in which they have any legislative functions; their knowledge of the wants of the church makes them valuable advisers on the principal committees of the benevolent boards.

There are two objections made to the power of the bishops:

First: Their absolute power of appointment.

Second: The power of their personal influence in the church.

Every intelligent man who has had any experience in business will concede the necessity of a directing head in the performance of important executive duties, and every observant man will acknowledge, as one of the defects of other church organizations, the absence of power to utilize to the best advantage their ministerial and other forces. In the practical working of their system of filling pulpits, the interest of but one church is consulted; the stronger churches select the ablest ministers, and to the weak churches are left the least desirable preachers, or they are left unsupplied. Such a system is narrow, and is not adapted to a vigorous and aggressive system.

The Methodist Episcopal Church is able, through the itinerancy, to supply every station, circuit, and mission work with a preacher, and all its preachers with employment in the work to which they have been called. To do this effectively, and with the least friction, the itinerancy and the sole power of appointment by a bishop are absolutely necessary. The Wesleyan method is defective in England, and would be impracticable in this country. As charges are made against the bishops in their use of this power, it is fair to ask, Wherein can a bishop unfairly use or abuse this trust? The answer will be, in unequally distributing the men to the work; in failing to recognize the claims of some and giving to others better appointments than they deserve; in having favorites, and in being unduly influenced by the advising elders. That the administration of the bishops may not be faultless is part of their humanity, and herein they are on the same footing with the objectors; but the experience of the church proves that, granting all possible and probable errors of judgment, the bishops, in the whole history of the church, have been singularly fortunate in the performance of their very delicate duties. This result is an evidence not so much of their human wisdom as of divine guidance. As an offset against error of judgment, or even intentional oppression, is the fact that such oppression can continue but one year; that is, until the meeting of the next Annual Conference, when, under the presidency of another bishop, wrongs may be redressed. Men rarely act oppressively or misuse power without an equivalent object in view. What object or interest can a bishop have in doing injustice in his appointments to either the ministers or the laity? On the one side, his natural sympathies are with his brethren of the ministry. If he has been a pastor,—and none other should be elected to the office of bishop,—he knows their peculiar trials and difficulties. Experience and observation teach him why and wherein certain characteristics of mind, manner, habits, ability, and acquirement in a preacher are best suited to the peculiar wants of a certain station or circuit. His chief business is to study these characteristics, and the wants of each station and circuit, and it is marvellous how rapidly a few years' service in the superintendency educates a bishop in this direction. In fine, the experience of Episcopal Methodism in this country has approved the itinerancy, and the necessity of the degree of power granted to the bishops.

The other objection is to the personal influence of the bishops in the church. This objection is so puerile as to be scarcely worthy of an answer. However, it may be said of the bishops, that if they had no influence upon the church they would be unworthy of their places; that their influence has been based on their wisdom and godly character; that it is the result of careful observation of their speech and conduct by the whole church, an ordeal few men can sustain; that no bishop has ever brought disgrace on himself, his fellows, or the church; and that the responsibilities they assume in their office have invariably made them better men. Where have been, and where are the men in the history of the church who were better entitled to exert all their personal influence than an Asbury, a McKendree, a George, an Andrew, a Janes, a Pierce, an Ames, a Simpson, or any of their fellow-bishops?

Some of the ministers will reply to this statement of the influence of the bishops by urging that there is another side that should be examined. They will assert that there has been, and that there is a constant tendency on the part of the bishops to secure and assume power through the influence of their position, as well as of their personality. Such a tendency is natural to men. It may be a praiseworthy ambition unduly extended. It is right and proper that such limitations should be placed upon their power as will secure the church from its abuse. These guards have been carefully established, as has been shown. The bishops can gain no more power unless with consent of the General Conference. To do this two things are required:

First: There must be unanimity of opinion among them as to the nature and extent of the desired increase of power; and,

Second: They must have the aid of the ministers to make the changes in the laws that are required to secure such power.

As to the first condition: The ministers should interrogate their candidates before election upon their ambitions, and obtain promises in advance as to their action. If there are any members of the present board, or if the General Conference should elect any hereafter, who sympathize with the fears of the brethren as to the tendency of the bishops to abuse or misuse their influence, they have an excellent opportunity to save the church from the threatened danger by simply refusing to become parties to such ambitious attempts. A minority of one may thus be as effective as a majority of the board. No increase of power can be secured without the assent of the whole board.

As to the second condition: The ministers can prevent such a dire catastrophe by embracing every opportunity of snubbing the bishops in the Conferences. They can show their independence, and exhibit their manliness of character and the sweetness of their tempers, by attacking them at all points, thereby reducing their influence, and so lessen any danger to the church. They can also instruct their delegates to vote against any such increase of power, whereby all danger will be at an end. But if ministers should become demoralized with the expectation of their own individual success, and be ready to grant a power they hope in time to exercise, where, then, is the church to look for succor? There are two safeguards that may be applied:

First: Greater care in the selection of the men for the office of bishop; and,

Secondly: By such an organization of the councils of the church as will introduce an element (laical) that will not be subject to the temptation or ambition to rule, and by such a distribution of power and responsibility as will enable this lay element to prevent any other order from gaining undue power or influence in the church. An application of these suggestions will prevent the bishops from misusing the influence that goes with their personal character and official position, and will protect the ministers from yielding to the temptation to assert for their order a power that does not belong to them. It will also protect them from the necessity of so continually reminding the bishops that they are men, and no better than their brethren of the same order, the elders; and, further, it will place on the laity the great charge to see that no harm comes to the church.

During the last General Conference there was an evident disposition among the ministry to express in some way their feeling of hostility to the bishops. There were two well-designed and judiciously-handled attacks upon them in that Conference. The first appears in taking advantage of a resolution expressive of the opinion of the Conference, that the Episcopacy is an office, not an order. The resolution was carried, and while many understood the object and what the effect would be, yet a majority feared to vote against it lest such vote should be misconstrued. The combination thereby gained one point, in making the false impression that such a resolution was required to keep the bishops from presuming that they were in any way superior in orders to the elders. It is a fair inference that the object of the resolution was to affect unfavorably the position of the bishops before the ministers and the members of the church, by creating an impression that such a grave deliverance was required to correct an existing opinion held by one or more of that body. Such a resolution might influence ministers, but would fail to affect the laity; for it is their pleasure to respect and reverence the bishops and to give them their fullest confidence. If this was not the intention, what was it? Was it a mere recitation of a well-established principle of our church government? If so, the resolution was superfluous. If any one of the bishops so thought, or if any of the members whom it was arranged to elect as bishops so believed, the passage of the resolution could have no influence on them. If such a deliverance had been placed in the ritual, so that the new men might be questioned as to their belief on this exceedingly important point of church government, then it would have gone for what it was worth; but we repeat that whatever may have been intended, the resolution had in it all the appearance of an understood attack on the bishops,—not personally, but upon the relation of a bishop to the church.

So much has been written about orders in the ministry, that a little attention to this subject may show wherein it may have an interest for some of the ministers.

The Methodist Episcopal Church provides for the two orders of deacon and elder in its ministry; these orders are patterned after what is believed to have been the relation held by men like Stephen, James, John, and others. It was a practical arrangement of work made to provide for the interests and growth of the young church. The one set of men are called deacons, the other elders. The church as a precautionary measure has provided certain tests before a man can become a deacon, and other tests of knowledge, character, acceptability, and piety, before he is admitted into the ministry as an elder. These precautionary requisitions are designed to guard against the introduction of improper or unprepared men into the ministry. They are altogether of human origin. The limited authority given to the exhorters, to the deacons, and the full authority given to the elders to perform certain duties, have the same origin. The authority to the elders to marry, to baptize, to administer the sacraments, to ordain other men to the ministry, is based on the fitness of things. Now, then, wherein does an order differ from an office which requires certain preparation, imposes certain duties, and grants certain powers? If there is any difference, it must arise from some peculiar power given to those holding an order, and which is denied to those who hold an office. It is at this point where the trouble comes in which has distracted the Church of Jesus Christ for more than fifteen hundred years. Without the shadow of reason, yet the word order has been used as a basis on which to erect all the splendid churches of the past, and many of the strong churches of to-day, this basis being that the word order includes the claim that special spiritual gifts accompany different orders. Those in the highest order receive the particular and peculiar power to perform all religious rites, such as marrying, baptizing, administration of the sacraments, control of the church, etc. This is of course equivalent to holding that some special divine gift is bestowed on the elders that is not given to the deacons or to the laity. This comparison of these claims as to the orders with the simple manner and object of their creation, is enough to expose their absurdity. There is something very pleasing and attractive to weak humanity in the word ORDER: it indicates rank not place, it makes the elders little popes, whom Monseigneur Capel would style as mere "imitators," as he does the

Ritualists in the English Church. Yet it is just at this point that so-called high-church opinions have a stronger hold on the ministry of the Methodist Episcopal Church than the members suppose, and these opinions, worthy of Rome and the English State Church, are largely at the root of the opposition of the ministers to lay representation.

The effort to humble the bishops by passing the resolution that they were not members of a special order, but were office-holders in the same order as their brethren, was evidently intended not to elicit a vote that the bishops were not superior in the Church of Christ to the deacons or to the laity, but that they were not the superiors in the church of the elders, of the ministerial members of the General Conference. This was the point which was supposed to touch their *amour propre*. The term "order" is generally used to express classes of men who have some special work, employment, or bond of association, or some distinguishing characteristic, as the Masonic Order, the Odd-Fellows, Order of Red Men, the Dominican, Jesuit, and other orders of the Roman Church. The same words are applied to deacons and elders, and in the general use of the term would include the bishops as an order, for they form a class.

The word "order" is, then, a general term applied to classes, while "office" is specific, as applied to the few. There can be no harm in saying either that the bishops are in a certain order, or that they hold office in an order. Both names may be applied to them and be consistent with the distinction used, unless there are some certain powers incident and affixed to certain orders, and these powers are communicated by supernatural agency, or are divinely conveyed in the process of ordination or consecration.

The advocates of such a resolution should not forget that the laity are not prepared to consent to their assumptions of special spiritual power or authority over them and the deacons of the church, though the *Christian Advocate*, as already quoted, says it is theirs "to command,"—a most offensive word. These brethren should remember, that the laity agree with the Rev. Dr. Stevens, that all the forms used in the Methodist Episcopal Church are for "decency's sake," and for the better and more seemly administration of the work of the church; it is the same reason that underlies all the forms used in civil governments. The laity believe in the inherent right of every Christian to do and perform any and every rite in the church, including the ordination or formal setting apart of men to any work. This last sentence is introduced with the object of correcting another error of our assuming elders, which is the making of a distinction between ordination and consecration. Deacons and elders are ordained to an order,—that is, simply set apart to do a certain work. This is, perhaps, as good a word as "assigned," as a form of words is part of the process. Business men "assign" men to do a certain work; this would convey the object of the process more clearly: but bishops go through a form of consecration by laying on of hands of elders. The use of this word to the ordinary man involves the idea that the candidate passes through a process of being made holy, either by some special transmission of grace from the Divine being through the hands of the elders, or by receiving such grace direct from such elders, either of which propositions is repugnant to the intelligence of the laity of the Methodist Episcopal Church.

It may be well at this place to notice the change of the Methodist Episcopal Church in its interpretation of what is done, conveyed, or imparted in the ordinance of consecration. The change was made by the General Conference of 1864.

Up to that time high-church ideas of prelatical transmission and reception of the Holy Spirit through the person (the hands) of those administering the ordinance of consecration prevailed. The fathers had copied the services of the English Church, and had taught the doctrine of the transmission of the Holy Ghost through the administrators, being the essence of the dogma of apostolic succession. The radical change thus taught will be readily seen by the following extracts from the Ritual.

Up to 1864 the form of words used was (the bishop and elders laying their hands upon the elected person): "Receive the Holy Ghost for the office and work of a bishop in the Church of God, now committed unto thee by the imposition of our hands, in the name of the Father, Son, and of the Holy Ghost. Amen. And remember that thou stir up the grace of God which is given thee by the imposition of our hands."

The General Conference of 1864 altered the wording to read, "The Lord pour upon thee the Holy Ghost for the work and office of a bishop in the Church of God, now committed unto thee by the authority of the church, through the imposition of our hands," etc., "and remember that thou stir up the grace of God that is within thee."

The form of ordination of elders was altered in 1792, from, " Receive the Holy Ghost for the office," etc., to, " The Lord pour upon thee the Holy Ghost for the office and work of an elder," etc.

This important change in the doctrine of the church has not had time to affect the views of the ministers educated to the former teachings.

The second attack on the Episcopacy was in the use made of the answer of the bishops to the request of the General Conference for their opinion upon the wisdom of electing a bishop for India. Independently of the question how far the bishops were correct in their opinion given to the General Conference, it was evidently a good time to lower the confidence with which their opinions, when asked for, had been received by preceding General Conferences.

The church at large may be congratulated on the failure of the attempt to secure a majority vote of the laity and the ministry against the bishops. The lay delegates wisely decided that the Board of Bishops (including the four who had been on the ground, and had carefully studied the wants of the work and its peculiarities) understood the inside and outside influences and movements connected with the question, the difficulties that would come to the Missionary Society if the proposition prevailed, and the dangers connected with it, to the church at home and in India. They believed that the Board of Bishops comprehended the question more thoroughly in all its bearings, and had better grounds on which to base an opinion, than the Missionary Committee or the members of the General Conference. And then again they were unwilling to aid the effort to humiliate the bishops in this direct attack on them, for, in the judgment of these iconoclasts, to weaken or destroy the confidence of the church in the bishops, individually and collectively, was evidently an important and necessary step in their aspirations. They feel that the bishops are in their way in their effort to gain the control of the church. Reference is only made to the devisers of the movement, not to all those who voted in favor of the proposition.

Again, an opportunity of belittling the bishops was eagerly seized on by some of the delegates, in their exceedingly discourteous, and unwise, and unjust refusal to extend to Bishop Wiley, who had been requested by the Conference to act as chairman of a special committee, the usual privilege given to the chairmen of committees to close a debate.

A third plan of this ministerial party is to limit the term of the bishops to four years,—from one General Conference to another. If this could be done, they see very clearly that the office or order of bishops would soon lose its influence and the respect and confidence of the church. Such a change would open the flood-gates of corruption upon the Conferences; the occupants of the office would in most cases be unworthy of the place, because good men would not submit to the conditions that would then elect them. These demoralizing influences would affect the ministers; the power of partisanship and the control of the bishops would drive upright men out of the ministry of the church; the management of the moneyed interests of the church boards and societies would suffer in the confidence of the people. The system of the itinerancy could not be carried on with bishops who would not be able in their four years of service to cover the whole territory of the church. Any defect at this point would seriously injure, and in the end destroy, the general polity of Methodism. The laity could not accept bishops so elected as proper arbitrators between them and the ministry. The great influence which is now exerted by the bishops in unifying the church in keeping up a general and common interest in all its parts would be destroyed.

The ultimate result of such a plan would be to divide the church into dioceses, with an elected president for each one,—an emasculated Methodism.

BY USE OF THE ANNUAL CONFERENCES.

A third direction in which the partisan ministers work to secure their object is by the passage of resolutions in the Annual Conferences instructing the bishops as to their administration, and in attempting by resolutions to forestall the opinion of the body of the church. It is an effort in which they hope that by some sort of *coup de main* they may get the advantage of a grave expression of the judgment of the fathers and brethren of a Conference in advance of action by the General Conference, or the formation of an opinion by the members. While these brethren ought to know that the opinions of the ministry in any church have less weight with their people, or with the public, than in former years, the causes of which it is not necessary to discuss, yet they also know that church opinion may be influenced by the action of an Annual Conference.

It is at this initial point that laymen should be present as members of Annual Conferences, and have a part in the formation of such utterances, if they are to be made. This argument deserves consideration; it will be a safeguard in the event of a contest between the ministers as against the bishops and the laity, which is inevitable unless stopped by the introduction of wise counsellors into our church bodies. Some of the Annual Conferences gravely assume the right to instruct the bishops as to their appointment of presiding elders, of preachers to stations, as to transfers, etc., and endeavor thus to influence the presiding officer in the performance of his duties. They hope, by this constant system of aggression, to gain the recognition of a right not only to pass such resolutions, but to give to them the force of instructions. They understand how assumption of power, unresisted, gradually comes to be acknowledged as a right. To meet such assertion of power it is very important for the safety of the church that the laity should be present in the Annual Conferences. The disgraceful scenes in the Philadelphia Annual Conference of 1884, when the bishops and laity were so bitterly attacked, will not soon be forgotten by the laymen who were present. If there was needed any additional argument in favor of the full introduction of lay representation in the Annual Conferences, it was such a scene. Any system of civil or church government which permits the members of a body to make such charges and aspersions against their equals without providing for a means of meeting them is grossly defective.

TRANSFERS.

Many of the ministers are led into a false position, indeed they fall into a trap shrewdly prepared by the leaders of the prelatical party in the church, by the arguments they use as to the respective rights of the Conferences and bishops in the matter of transfers. The simplest statement of their argument being, that the appointment to charges in a Conference primarily belongs to the members of such Conference, and therefore, unless there are not enough men to meet the demand, no transfer should be made, and if made, such transfers should be appointed to the less desirable stations or circuits. Such a plain statement of the case will not be acceptable to some ministers, as it reveals ignorance of the law of the church and intense selfishness, with a large degree of personal vanity, because such transfers are usually appointed to the more desirable charges.

The *first* assumption is: That membership in a Conference carries with it some special power or rights that are inherent in the Conference. The *second:* That one of these rights is a preference in the appointments for such Conference. The *third:* That there are in each Conference ministers fully able to take charge of and sustain any pulpit in such Conference.

The thorough baselessness of the first and second assumptions has been, hereinbefore, so fully exposed that it is not necessary now to more than allude to some of the arguments then made, viz.: First: That every minister in the Methodist Episcopal Church is a member of the church at large, and should receive his appointment solely in view of the good and the requirements of the general work. Second: The subdivision of the general work into Annual Conferences and presiding elders' districts is purely one of convenience in administration, without detriment to or affecting the true relation of a minister to the church at large. To argue otherwise is to deny to every minister in the church his right to the appointment in the gift of the bishops wherein he can be of the most service to the cause of Christ. Such a denial would be destructive of the essence of the itinerancy, and of the most important work of a bishop, which is to find the preacher, anywhere in the country, who may be the best adapted to the wants of any special mission, church, or district wherever it may be located. These statements are enough for the law of the case; neither the ministers nor the laymen should be willing to give up this essential feature of the itinerancy. It is almost the Magna Charta of their rights in the church.

The use of the word transfer is, strictly speaking, a misnomer, at least in its generally accepted sense; the man is not transferred and then appointed: but first appointed and then transferred. The true theory should not be forgotten, that an appointment is first made by the bishop: and then, for the convenience of administration, such appointee is enrolled in the list of a certain Annual Conference, which embraces the church, station, or district to which he is appointed. He is not transferred to a Conference,* but appointed to work in the bounds of a Conference; and further, that an Annual Conference is in the nature of a commission created by the General Conference for certain purposes, and at its annual meeting the ministers who are connected with the commission receive their appointments for the year following.

The causes of the existence of the feeling against transfers in many Conferences are worth analyzing. Offensive odors generally indicate decay. Complaints by the ministers of a want of appreciation by the people show very clearly the good sense of the people in discerning the lazy, the indolent, the old sermons, and the lifeless manner. Among the objectors to transfers may be found those for whom the bishops have great trouble in finding places by reason of lack of confidence of their brethren in them, of want of ability or usefulness, and some for reasons not necessary to mention. Then, too, there is a class of the ministers already alluded to who are full of vanity and self-esteem: they think if the system of transfers was stopped there would

---

* The recently adopted plan of the bishops, in first making the transfer and leaving the appointment to the bishop presiding, cannot nullify the principle in the polity of the church. As among themselves, the reasons for such a change are obvious.

be less sending of first-class men to third-class appointments; and they would be personally benefited. The plain facts in the case are ignored: no church would ask for a transfer if it could be as acceptably served at home; the churches may err, but it is their best judgment, and if the bishop, presiding elder, and the minister in question agree with them that the transfer may be the best thing to be done, that should be the end of it. The wisest precautions have been taken; the church can provide no more. It is certainly a safer plan than to take the judgment of an aspiring minister as to his qualifications for an appointment. There are among us many men of God who are thankful that they are deemed worthy of being sent to any place to preach Christ and him crucified, and to tell others what he has done for them; and again there are others who do not sympathize with such sentiments; they desire to select the dying men to whom they may preach their gospel. There are several influences that create a feeling of opposition to transfers among good men. Some of these have their origin in the facts, That by reason of the small difference in the majority of the ministry as to pulpit ability, usefulness, and acceptability, the bishops have used the power of transfer to a very limited extent; that a long residence in a Conference begets personal and family attachments; that with increasing age comes hesitation and unwillingness to risk change of people, of habits, and of country. Ministers who have been raised within the boundaries of a Conference that has for years retained its name, like the Philadelphia or the Baltimore Conferences; who have entered the ministry in connection therewith, have married and have their family interests within its boundaries, do not feel that they can, without much discomfort and inconvenience to themselves and families, and perhaps pecuniary loss, be transferred to another Conference.

They therefore hold on, take appointment after appointment, each within hearing distance of the other, and the result is that they find even in middle life, and though they may be industrious, studious, hard-working, faithful, and good men, that their acceptability is waning. They see others transferred to pulpits they hoped to fill, and the future begins to appear dark; how readily are such men tempted to look at the wrong cause and the wrong remedy! The cause is in themselves. It is in the simple fact that any minister will lose his acceptability and usefulness (especially a Methodist minister) whose voice, manner, and current of thought become familiar to a people. The remedy is the freer use of the power of transfer, with all its accompanying disabilities and drawbacks. Yet these embarrassments would in the end cause less pain and less self-denial to the minister and his family, through the gain of an extended time of usefulness and the ability to earn a comfortable support.

Another reason that influences many of the ministry is due to their financial interests in the several aid societies with which they may have been connected for a long time, which would be lost or impaired by a transfer.

Three other thoughts are worthy of consideration:

First: The good influence of transferred men on the

ministry and people to whom they are sent. It is like the introduction of new blood to an old family; it gives a sparkle to the life that was lost; it is apt to push aside grooved thoughts and ways; it prevents the effeteness that accompanies uninterrupted manners and customs, and, more than that, it insures a unity in the church. It develops men; a new people will waken a slow man and stir up a sluggish one.

Second: In this wide country our people are seldom brought into contact on church interests, and the tendency will be to create different phases of Methodism in different parts of the country. A more general exchange of ministers will do much towards making the church homogeneous, and thereby help to counteract the disintegrating tendencies of separated church life. These influences are noticeable in Eastern Methodism, the Methodism of the Middle States, of the South, and of the West.

Third: There is something to be learned from the experience of other churches. In no other church is there anything of the narrowness that would prevent any minister in any part of the country from accepting a pastorate in any other part of the country. What would be thought of a Presbytery, a Council, a Diocesan Convention refusing to accept a minister from another like body by reason of its location? They fully recognize the fact that ministers soon lose their influence over a people, and so they rarely change from one church to another in the same city or district, but seek for a pastorate among a new people in a different part of the country.

It is to be hoped, for the honor of the Methodist Episcopal Church, that the ministers will overrule all attempts to destroy the rights of their brethren, if they do not value their own rights; all attempts to ignore a vital principle of the itinerancy; or to interfere with the advantage the system of transfers secures to the ministers and their families, and the influence it has on the unity of the church.

THE PRESIDING ELDERS.

Reference has been made to the effort, in the interest of the class-feeling among the ministry, to change the relation, in the organization of the church, of the presiding elders to the bishops. It may not therefore be amiss to refresh the minds of some of the members by a glance at the present relation of the elders to the bishops and to the church, and their peculiar duties.

They are appointed by a bishop presiding at an Annual Conference to take charge of the interests of the church in a particular district of country. It is their duty to report to and consult with the bishop in charge as to such interests, and to attend the bishop when in their districts. At the Annual Conferences they more formally report not only upon the general interests, but upon the special interests of each charge and the work of each minister in their districts. They may be appointed to a district for four successive years, but an interval of six years must elapse before they can be reappointed to the same district.

Their duties to the church are varied, including the holding of a Quarterly Conference at each station or circuit every three months, at which time the detailed interests of such station or circuit are canvassed; they have control of the elders, deacons, travelling and local preachers and exhorters in their districts; they are charged with overseeing "the spiritual and temporal" business of the church, with looking after the general collections for the church boards; they may change, receive, and suspend preachers during the interval between the sessions of a Conference and in the absence of a bishop; they decide all questions of law in a Quarterly Conference. It is their duty to look after the young men who contemplate entering the ministry, and by their fatherly advice guide them in the way of preparation.

This sketch of their duties will reveal, to many who may not have carefully read the Discipline, that the presiding elders occupy a very important place in carrying out the polity of the church; they are sub-bishops or superintendents of their districts, many of which are quite as large and important as some of the dioceses in the Episcopal Church. The value of their work in the older Conferences may not be so apparent. It is necessary that a useful machine should first be well built; secondly, be carefully watched; and, thirdly, have a competent machinist at hand in case of need. So with the organization and administration of the elders' districts. The organization is unexceptionable: a competent elder will carefully watch its working, and be ready with a remedy in case of need. The machinery of the church needs no regulation while working smoothly; it does require careful watching, it does at times require the presence and power of an elder, to preserve it from harm. The perfection of an organization is seen when it seems to work by its own inherent power. The duties of the eldership require men of trained minds, good judgment, prudence, pulpit ability, and administrative talent. In the earlier days such men were carefully selected; they became leaders, and exercised great influence within the church and on the people of the districts which they travelled; they were a recognized power in Methodism and in the country.

In the olden time, and even yet in some places, the approach of the Quarterly Conference and the coming of the elder were and are looked forward to as times of a gracious outpouring of the Holy Spirit, of the gathering in of the members of a circuit for religious worship, of the hospitable provision for all comers, of the initiated revival, and the strengthening of the feeble churches. While the office of a presiding elder has been acknowledged as a necessity in the past for the successful working of the organization of the church, it is evident that the future demands of the church will require its continuance, and that it shall be filled by the highest style of men in the ministry. Its importance will increase in proportion to the growth of the church, the development of its interests, and the inability of the bishops to maintain that knowledge of the ministers and their work which they did in past years. The work of a bishop is changing in this respect; he must now depend very largely on the suggestions and information given by the elders, on their wisdom, prudence, tact, and knowledge of the men and the people.

The eldership excited at an early day great hostility, and various efforts were made to limit the powers and duties of the office. At first this was due to the continued appointment of the same men as elders, and much of the opposition was engendered because it was felt by some of the preachers that their claims were overlooked; that there was favoritism exercised. Now the claim is, not that the office shall be dispensed with, for its importance to the work of the church is too evident, but that the power of appointment by the bishop shall be limited to a selection from some fixed number of preachers nominated by the members of an Annual Conference, or that the elders shall be elected by the Conferences, or that they—the Conferences—shall have an authoritative voice in the appointments, or in some way break the exclusive power of appointment by the bishops, and thus enable the ministers to partition the appointments among themselves. Some of these objections have been elsewhere discussed; they are noted at this point to open the way for a consideration of the policy of granting the right to the Annual Conferences to interfere with or to change the present relation of the bishops to the elders, to the ministry, and to the laity, and the results should such change take place.

The granting of such power to an Annual Conference, or the making of any changes in the organization of the church which would interfere with the appointing by the bishop, either of elders or preachers, would be in the line not of administration only, but of legislation. This power has been shown in the discussion of the Annual Conference to be impracticable and entirely inconsistent with proper government. The Annual Conferences were instituted for special purposes, and legislative powers are inconsistent with the object of their creation. Again, the granting of such power would be in violation of the relation that exists, by virtue of the organization of the church, between the ministry, the laity, and the bishops; it would be introducing an element which would destroy the balance now existing. For the good of the church the ministry agree to go wherever sent by the bishops, and the laity agree to receive whomsoever the bishops may send. Any other power than that of a bishop, who is independent of both parties and a just arbitrator, would be properly resisted. The proposed interference with this power of the bishops would destroy the itinerancy.

From the fact of the presence of the bishop, as in some sense an arbitrator, arises the right of both parties to meet him and give him the benefit of their views as to the appointment to be made to any particular station. This is especially the right of the laity, because of the elders acting as advisers of the bishop. If the laity were not so recognized they would be helpless against either a body of elders or even one elder, who for any reason unwisely or unjustly opposed their wishes as to who should be their minister. The proposition to introduce laymen into the councils of the bishops as an offset to the influence of the elders would increase the difficulties that now exist; the laymen are not prepared or fitted to undertake such a duty. Again, the essence of good administration is found in securing a proper responsibility. If the elders are forced on the bishops by nomination or by election, there will be a destruction of responsibility. The bishops are responsible to the General Conference for their administration, they could not be held responsible for the actions of men they did not choose; the elders are not now and could not be made answerable to the General Conference for their advice to the bishops. The wisdom of the present policy of allowing the bishops to choose their advisers is further shown by the fact that it is the policy adopted in all governments. All constitutional governments give either their presidents or the prime minister this power; it is a recognized necessity to secure good administration and proper responsibility. The delicate and responsible duties to be performed by the bishops in determining the appointments render their power of appointing the elders the more proper and necessary. Indeed, all restrictions as to reappointments of elders should be erased from the Discipline. They found their way into it from petty jealousy, envy, unworthy ambition, and with but little cause. The bishop should have unrestrained access to the best advice from the most competent elders, in addition to the information to be gained from the laity, from intercourse with the people, from observation, and from his colleagues.

A most potent argument against changing any part of the present law respecting the presiding elders, their power and duties, and their relation to the ministry, will be found in the trouble that would come with it to the ministry. Introduce the right to nominate, to elect, or to give the elders the power of a veto upon the bishops, and the flood-gates of bargain and sale, of corrupt engagements, of contracts, deals, and understandings, would be let in upon the Conference, to the disgust of all good men and the demoralization of the ministry. It would at once introduce discord between the ministry and the laity, for the laity could not, with any self-respect, submit their interests in the church to a council so composed.

Let, then, the presiding eldership be kept as it is, but let more care be taken by the bishops in selecting the elders. The interests of the church require the choice of a higher class of men than is the case in many of the Annual Conferences.

TERM OF SERVICE.

The class power of the ministry is proposed to be strengthened by a prolongation of the term of service. The well-known opposition to it by the laity, as expressed in the lay vote in the last General Conference, furnished an additional argument to some of the ministry why an increase in the lay representation should be prevented. An element of safety at this point is found in the facts that the advocates of a longer term are not found among the more acceptable and intelligent of the ministers, and that they are not largely represented in a General Conference.

With a due regard to the drawbacks and sacrifices of the itinerancy, yet what other system will insure a minister as prolonged and useful a life, as long a term of service, or a better support? There are involved in it personal considerations, and it is not suited to every man who may feel it his duty to preach. With this class there is no place for argument. If there are men in the ministry of the Methodist Episcopal Church who are not in sympathy with the principles of its polity, and feel that they can be more useful to the cause of Christ in working under some other organization, it is far better for them, and it will be to the advantage of the church, that they withdraw their membership. There is no disgrace connected with such withdrawal. All reasonable men will recognize the fact that no system of church government is exactly adapted to all. Each has its peculiarities, and it is largely as men can harmonize their thoughts, feelings, and habits with such peculiarities that they should make church connections and associations. The prayers and good will of the church should go with all such brethren. There is more of Christian manhood in thus withdrawing, when the minister finds himself unsuited to the itinerancy, than there is in remaining in the church as a continual grumbler, and striving to change its laws to suit his own preferences. There are drawbacks connected with, and personal sacrifices to be made in, the Methodist ministry; there is no situation in life of which the same may not be written, and there are no more of such hindrances to comfort and the enjoyment of personal desires in the Methodist ministry than in any other calling. Every station and condition in life has drawbacks peculiar to itself.

Not infrequently a minister is heard complaining of

his support, and declaring how much more money he could have made if he had engaged in worldly pursuits. This is finding fault with his Master for calling him to preach, and not to make money. Such complaints and such an argument indicate either a mistake on the part of the man in supposing he was called to preach, or that his love has grown cold and that his interest in his Master's cause is waning. Sad, indeed, is it for any one who has been really called to follow, not only in the footsteps of the Apostles, but in those of Christ, to fall so low. Such men should at once withdraw from the ministry.

There is another suggestion to be made to such brethren,—that those who thus complain seem to have a wrong view of the theory of the Methodist Episcopal Church as to the object of the pay they receive from the members. Such complainants accept the pay as hire for their services, which, if sold in the labor market, they say, would bring them much larger returns. These brethren should understand that the Methodist Episcopal Church is as much opposed to a "hireling ministry" as the "Friends." The church would not dare to estimate the value of the services of an efficient minister. The reward for such services is to be measured and accounted for hereafter by the great Head of the church. While here, the church only promises the best support that can be obtained while the ministers are engaged in persuading men to be saved, in showing them that their souls are immortal and above price, that they cost the life of Jesus Christ, the Son of God. Who, then, would dare place a money value on the worth of a human soul? Who would estimate, by money, the value of the work of an Asbury, a Maffitt, a Simpson, a McClintock, or the work of any earnest minister of Jesus Christ?

Some of our ministers seem to grow thin in spirit and flesh through dissatisfaction with their calling, while the fathers, with real discomfort and with great sacrifices, grew strong in spirit, "making mirth," as Rouse has it, and gained flesh as well. But, granting all that may be urged about the sacrifices demanded of the ministry by the itinerancy, it amounts to this: If the greatest amount of good can be done in this way, if it is the best use of the material, then Christ's cause being so far above human complaints or inconveniences, such complaints have no place in the argument, but must be regarded as entirely secondary and subordinate. Before proceeding in the discussion of this question of the extension of time it may be well to understand that while propositions have been made for an extension of time, such cases have been urged as exceptional, to be used only in certain emergencies, or to meet peculiar wants. Let not the church be deceived by such a statement. The same argument was used at the time of the extension to three years, and it immediately became the rule so far as it could be made, the ministers feeling aggrieved if not returned to a station the third time; they make three years the rule, less time the exception; so it will be with any increase of time.

In analyzing the wisdom of a prolonged term of service, it will be found to depend on the characters of the answers to two questions. First: How will any extension of time affect the principle of the itinerancy? Second: How would such extension of time affect the ministers of the church, their usefulness and acceptability?

In the answers to these questions will be found the true solution of a problem which is so deeply agitating the minds of some of the ministry.

First, then, the principle of the itinerancy is well understood as being the securing of the services of the ministers for the largest number of places in the country without regard to number of members, location, climate, health, or means of support, and the highest average of ability, in all respects, for all places. Any change which would limit the ability of the bishops to supply with preachers the smallest number of people, the poorest and most ignorant of the race, in the most distant section of country, in the least desirable climate, in the most unhealthy places, and with the most uncomfortable surroundings, would be an invasion of the principle of the itinerancy, and would affect the efficiency of the church to the extent of such inability. While there may be but few places in the older Conferences which could not be supplied if a longer term of service was allowed, yet the fact that the people of any section of any Conference would be left unsupplied is a sufficient argument against a change of time.

Many ministers in the older Conferences are even now unwilling to go for even one or two years to the unhealthy places, to hard appointments, to a lowly and humble people, and to a poor and uncertain support.

They plead their families' needs, their personal preferences, they urge that they are prepared to fill better appointments, that it would be a humiliation to them to be sent to such charges, that it would lower their Conference position among their brethren, and would operate against their future elevation. It is this kind of objections and pleas, this sort of failure to measure up to the mark of a true minister, to properly value the honor and duty of his calling, to imitate the Master and His apostles and disciples, who went about among the lowly doing good, healing the sick, giving sight to the blind, and making the lame and the halt leap for joy; it is this class of objections, it is repeated, that gives the bishops much of their trouble in assigning men to appointments. It is at this point, too, where dissatisfaction takes its rise, and herein is the foundation of many of the complaints about transfers, and the demand for an extension of time.

In some of the older Conferences there may be a higher average of desirability in the stations and circuits, yet in the majority of the Conferences there are many places which are not supplied with preaching; many poor people who can give but little; and many unhealthy and undesirable districts. Wherever a family or a settlement is made in this vast country with its rapidly-increasing population, is found a place for a Methodist itinerant to preach the gospel. There is just as much need, taking the country as a whole, for the retention of the ability to supply all such places as there ever was, probably more, estimating the extent of country settled and the number of its population.

This question of extension of time must be judged as a whole for the whole church and all the country. Though it were possible that a prolongation of time might not materially decrease the efficiency of the itinerancy in certain parts of the older Conferences, where its spirit is almost extinguished, yet if such extension of service is not applicable to the whole church, it should not be accepted.

The self-denial herein demanded of the ministers is in principle the same kind of sacrifice, if it can be so called, that is now made by the laymen in giving up the services of the more acceptable ministers that weaker appointments may have the advantage of their labors, and that the full benefits of the itinerancy may be enjoyed by the members in all sections of our country. It cannot be denied that the adoption of the three years' limit has increased the difficulty of reaching scattered populations, unhealthy districts, and weak charges, even in the older Conferences, and it is a fair inference that the longer the time the greater will be this difficulty.

This experience should be sufficient to rule out all applications for increased time, however strong and conclusive other arguments may be.

But the extension of time would operate against the second cardinal point in the Methodist organization,— the securing a better average of preaching in all the appointments. While it is true there seems to be a certain general level of ability in the pulpit, because the natural ability of men does not greatly vary, yet there is a sufficient variety in peculiar lines that makes frequent changes desirable and useful. Some are mighty in exhortation, in gathering in from the world; others in building up the believers; others in their personal influence, and so on. Adding together these varied characteristics of eight or ten Methodist preachers in a continuous service of from twenty to thirty years at any one station, and it will produce a sum of ability to reach and influence for good a greater number of people than is possible to the average men in the ministry of any church, if not to the most gifted men.

A failure for the future in these two great results of the itinerancy in the past would be destructive of the life and spirit of Methodism. The laity understand this; they have borne with the last change patiently; they will not accept any further extension of time.

The second test of this question of extension of time will be considered,—viz., its effect on the usefulness and acceptability of the ministry of the church. While it is acknowledged that length of service is, in a sense, arbitrary, that it should be suited to circumstances, and may be judged by its influence on the capacity of the church to reach the people everywhere, and to give the highest average of ministerial service, yet it is fair to consider these points in connection with the number, character, natural ability, acquirements, and piety of the men who are to do the work.

The ministers must accept the judgment of the laity as to these points; they are unfit judges of their own ability, wisdom, character, piety, usefulness, and acceptability. These matters affect too closely their personal appreciation, preferences, and family interests.

Public teachers are very apt to overestimate themselves at all these points, more particularly their ability in the pulpit, their judgment, acceptability, and usefulness. Ministers of all the churches are subject to this criticism. There will be a wide difference in the number of Pauls, of Apolloses, of Johns, and of Peters in the ministry, according as taken at the estimate of the individual ministers or that of their hearers.

It is but fair to consider the arguments some of the ministers use in favor of increased length of service, so that, with the whole subject before the church, a fair conclusion may be reached upon the wisdom of any change. The principal arguments used, leaving out purely personal considerations, are two:

First: That a minister can, in many instances, be more useful when stationed for four, five, six, or more years, than he can when limited to a term of three. To secure care and protection at this point, these brethren suggest that, in all cases of extension beyond the three years, the appointment shall meet the approval of the Quarterly Conference, of the Annual Conference, and of the presiding bishop, thus uniting the will or wish of the members and the judgment of the Annual Conference with that of the elders and bishop. With what seeming innocency do these ministers link the Conferences with the bishops, making them part of the appointing power!

Secondly: That our church loses in prestige and influence in our large cities through the ministers being removed before they can gain a proper position before the public.

To help answer these two arguments, and to more clearly comprehend the whole question of ministerial usefulness, it may be well somewhat critically to analyze the elements of the power of the ministers of the Methodist Episcopal Church, and again to refer to some of the causes of their success. Methodism has been called Christianity in earnest. This was the chief characteristic of its preaching in the past, is to a great extent to-day, and on its continuance depends much of its usefulness. It is said that these preachers produced their results by exciting the emotions and by appealing to the passions of rude people, and that such influences produced many of the extraordinary scenes of the past. Those who say this have little knowledge of the forces in human nature; they forget the character and condition of the people on whom such effects were produced. The sparsely-settled country, the felt influence of the infidelity of the times, the demoralization consequent on the revolutionary struggle and a continuous warfare with the Indian tribes, the general ignorance as to Christian teachings, the limited opportunities of hearing the gospel preached, the infrequent meetings for religious services, the lack of religious reading, the scarcity of the Bible,—these and other causes prepared all classes of the people, from the highest to the lowest, from the most learned to the most ignorant, for the effects produced by the earnest and plain preaching of the Methodist itinerants. It may be true that such results were more general among the rude and illiterate, who, when their eyes were opened by stirring exhortations and vivid descriptions to see their condition before God, acted naturally and without the restraints that the religious dilettante would impose upon them; they sought with loud cries and tears and found peace within their souls; the lions and tigers became as lambs, and little children could lead and teach them.

It is a proud boast of Methodism that it has preached the gospel to all peoples, and that the Spirit of God has owned its work in raising up men and women from the lowest as well as from the highest classes. The first object with the Methodist preacher has always been to save the soul, the Spirit working with it as it might. If the heart is thoroughly changed, it matters little as to the influence of personal characteristics in the struggle for pardon, or the method or manner of the expression of joy in the knowledge of such change, through the witness of the Holy Spirit.

The Methodist ministers have combined arguments with their appeals, but their arguments on religious questions have been rather inferences drawn from the teachings of faith. The religion of Jesus Christ cannot be defended by human reasoning; its foundation is faith. Man cannot comprehend the origin of creation, of his own being, the existence of God, or the mysteries of the Triune God, the method of the presence and influence of the Holy Spirit, the origin of life, nature and effects of death, of the resurrection. Man knows nothing of itself; he notes results, and sometimes thinks he reasons. The religion of Jesus Christ is founded on faith in the word of God. The teacher of this word is limited to persuading men to be reconciled according to the terms of faith in God. Man must be taught that to live with Christ here is the best, the truest life. The power of the preacher is displayed in his portraying the love of the Father, of Jesus Christ, His Son, and of the Holy Spirit for man. Love is built upon faith and trust, not on reason. Every one should feel thankful to God that when his reasoning reaches its maximum of power without satisfying the soul, faith is given to solve our problems.

The gospel of Christ is one of reconciliation, of love. The minister's appeals are therefore to the heart. This is the best and truest part of man; his reason may lead him astray; the affections are more reliable, the instincts are more true, and on the cultivation of the affections is to be built up Christian character, as well as all other character. All successful ministers have had the power of sympathetic connection with their hearers. Men are brought to Christ through their hearts, and not through their heads. This kind of preaching has characterized Methodist ministers, and, though many of them have been as learned as other ministers, they have generally held fast to this theory of successful preaching; and when they have abandoned it, in whole or in part, and assumed the argumentative and learned-essay style, their success has diminished. There may be a temptation to young men to appear learned in the pulpit and to ignore the experience of their fathers; older men should not yield to it.

Then, again, there are among the Methodist ministers a great many who are not learned, and who cannot produce well-written essays on moral subjects to be delivered to their people; when they attempt this they fail. But they can tell their religious experience, and perhaps weave the words of Charles Wesley's hymns into heart melodies, and thereby do good.

Again, the people expect the Methodist minister to do his best in every sermon, and the same degree of effort must go with him into the class-meeting, the prayer-meeting, and into all the church services; and this is one reason why the average preaching in the Methodist Churches is better and more effective than in any other church. There may be more learning in the Presbyterian pulpit, but it lacks the fire, the *élan*. The expression of this fire and *élan* is exhaustive of the nervous system; it exposes a man's inner life, character, and his powers of mind more quickly to a people than the reading of many beautiful homilies on religion. The Methodist pulpit is therefore more trying to the minister than any other. The members are accustomed to this kind of preaching; they are not content with anything less, and this is one point in which the argument in favor of extension of time drawn from prolonged service of ministers in other churches fails. The style and character of the preaching which prevails in other religious churches will not be accepted by Methodist people. There are but few men in the ministry of any church who can do this kind of work and keep up a full interest for more than two or, at the outside, three years. There is scarcely a minister in any evangelical church in the cities of Boston, New York, Philadelphia, or Baltimore who could fully sustain himself for more than three years in a Methodist pulpit.

As soon as the range of a preacher's mental powers, character of thought, arguments, and sympathetic nature is measured by a people, his usefulness is so nearly at an end that they look forward to the next Annual Conference for another victim of their exhausting and exacting demands. It is in this way that the Methodist ministry is kept at its best work, the closest to its abilities; and it is due to these demands that so many become unacceptable at an early age. If it were not for the short term of an appointment from year to year, an enforced supernumerary relation would be visited upon many more of the ministers. When a preacher ceases to improve in knowledge, grace, and interest in saving souls, he has no proper place in the ministry of the Methodist Episcopal Church. If, then, the time should be lengthened, its consequential results, decreased efficiency and loss of energy, must be met; the character and grade of service in the pulpit must be lowered to that of other pulpits, and with such lowering of standard much of the glory of Methodism will depart. It may hang its harps on the willows, for the strings that made such sweet sounds will have broken.

The argument used for extension of time in particular cases has, of course, some force, but, as has been noticed, there is always a practical difficulty in making general laws suit special cases, as the tendency is to make all cases special, which would be destructive of the object and principle of the law. The Roman

Catholic Church has an advantage in its organization from the fact that the priests being unmarried, their length of service is more readily determined by their success, the time of service being exclusively in the control of the bishop. The use of such arbitrary power is out of the question in the Methodist Church; even the present law in the Discipline recognizing special cases has had its fruit in unsettling the minds of some of the ministers. If such special cases were confined to those where unusually hard and undesirable work was to be done, with little pay, there might be less injury, for there would be fewer applicants.

An argument frequently used in favor of a longer term of service is that that the present limit of time deprives a church of the advantages connected with a settled pastorate, in the personal influence of the pastor over the members and their families, and more particularly over the young in the church. This argument is worthy of consideration.

Much of this idea of the power and benefit of pastoral influence is drawn from the recollection or historical handing down of the relation of the New England pastor of days long gone by to his people and their families. Whatever may be the cause, yet such a relation is now the exception; the instances of long-settled pastorates in any church are rare, and are decreasing in number. The average length of pastoral service is said not to exceed four to five years in the Presbyterian and Congregational Churches, five years in the Episcopal, and four years in the Baptist Churches. Counting the time lost in selecting a pastor, and the loss of pastoral influence during a disaffection until a change comes, and the useful period of a pastor's stay in any of these churches is greatly lessened, not averaging at most over three years.

The average time given for personal influence in these churches is not, therefore, more than in a term of three years in a Methodist Church, and the comparison of work performed is in favor of the Methodist preacher. The called preacher needs time to smooth down opposition, to become acquainted with his people. His work is laid out as if his new charge was to be a continuing home, and one or more years slip away before he gets fully into it, while the Methodist preacher knows that at most he has but three years in which to serve a church, and must therefore do his best from the first sermon. The social habits of the Methodist people are such as to make the preacher feel quickly at home, and the work goes on without interruption. The Methodist Episcopal Church, in its early organization, made provision to meet the loss of pastoral service by placing this duty on the class-leaders. All the members being enrolled in some class, each one was under the special pastoral supervision of his class-leader, thereby providing for the pastoral care of the flock while the preacher was engaged in evangelistic labors. This is another instance of the wonderful adaptation of the economy of the Methodist Episcopal Church to circumstances. In the theory of the church the class-leaders are, if not the pastors, the sub-pastors of every station or circuit.

The increase of stations and the decrease of circuits

in the older Conferences now enable the preachers in charge to do most of the pastoral work, and therefore the use of the leaders in this respect is not so general; but in large parts of our field the original and theoretical plan and policy of the church are continued.

After these statements it may be asked, Wherein would the members gain the benefit of a more perfect pastoral influence by the extension of the time of service? What advantages in this direction would such extension secure to the church?

Unless there was some assurance that the ministers of the Methodist Episcopal Church would be retained in an appointment for as long as, or for a longer time than the average of the term of service of the pastors of other churches, it would be unwise to base any church laws on a mere possibility. The results of experience must be taken as the foundation of law and administration. Experience certainly teaches that the time of the long pastorates has passed away, and for some of the reasons that have made the short pastorates in the Methodist Episcopal Church so successful; that the controlling influence of the pastors of a former day over a people and over the young no longer prevails; that the average length of an active pastorate is no longer than the term of the majority of Methodist preachers.

The questions asked may, in view of these facts, be answered by the fair inferences, that the length of service of the Methodist pastors, whatever the law may be, would not exceed the average length of the services of the ministers of other churches; that while the other churches are limited to one pastor, and when the pulpit is vacant are without any pastor, the provisions of the Methodist Episcopal Church supply a church at all times with at least one chief pastor and one, two, three, four, or more sub-pastors in the class-leaders; that the experience of other churches in securing the benefits of prolonged pastoral influence offers no proper reasons or inducements for any change in the term of service in the Methodist Episcopal Church.

If the policy of the church is faithfully followed, there will be no necessity that provision should be made for the special instances where an increase of time might aid the pastor in taking care of the fruits of a revival or the completion of improvements. The church has made ample provision for such cases. The defect is in the men who may fail to use them. Human laws are imperfect: they are made to cover and secure the best average of results. It is only Divine wisdom that can provide for every interest. Perfection is an attribute of Divinity only, not of man.

The argument that the Methodist Episcopal Church loses her proper influence in large cities and communities from the short term of service deserves notice. This argument is attractive because it appeals so directly to the vanity of many men, who at once fancy themselves as settled pastors in important churches in some large city; forgetting, or perhaps not being conscious of the fact that they have probably served no church for three years where the membership were not willing to exchange their services for those of another pastor. The influence of the minister as such,—however noted he may be for ability or idiosyncrasies of mind and manner—on public thought, opinion, and action, is steadily decreasing, not on account of the increased ungodliness of the people, but by reason of their increased intelligence and piety. The same reason affects the social and church influence of the ministers. In the former days the minister was the one highly-educated man in a parish, and his people listened with amazement at the learning shown in his Sunday tussles with dogmatic theology. Teaching and exhortation in practical theology are now demanded; these require more grace and true power in the preacher, and any failure therein is readily apprehended by his hearers. The influence of Methodist preaching has been potent in producing this change in the demands of other churches, with the result of decreased length of service in the Presbyterian, Congregational, Episcopal, and other churches. If these churches adopt Methodist usages, should not Methodists hesitate before changing their laws to suit the policy which other churches are abandoning?

The argument from personal influence has less force, because there are few ministers who are head and shoulders above their fellows, and who acquire more than a strong influence in their own church. An error is apt to be made as to the extent of the direct personal influence of leading ministers in cities. The minister represents an individual church or denomination, and his influence on the public is largely as the representative of the opinion and position of the members of the church he represents. As they have social standing, high moral reputation, public confidence, so will the influence of the minister be increased or decreased. Public opinion is made by the laity of the church. Finally, to meet the few instances where prolonged service might be advantageous and acceptable to the laity of any particular station would scarcely warrant a change in the laws of the church. Better for the Methodist Episcopal Church, if we have ministers who would acquire so great influence as settled pastors, that they should locate or resign and accept the pastorate of independent churches. The argument drawn from the gain to the church from such settled pastorates is very illusory. Mere worldly renown is not what a church should seek; it can have no higher honor than to have its efforts recognized and blessed by Christ. Ministers noted for oratory or for peculiarities, such as Beecher and Talmage, will attract strangers to a church and may do them good; but if a minister has such gifts, he will attract more hearers from outside of the church in an itinerant pastorate than when settled; he then comes as a fresh man with a high reputation to a new people, and in the end will do more good.

There are but few ministers in any denomination who have a national reputation; their influence extends but little beyond the people to whom they preach. Many able men who under the itinerancy would have had a widely-extended reputation are buried in a settled pastorate until the vigor of life is past and the ability to impress their hearers is gone. The settled pastorate does not develop men; by necessity such pastors fall into a humdrum manner and a stereotyped style of preaching. This is felt by many of the ministry and laity of such churches, and they would fain adopt some way of securing regular changes and more constant employment for their ministry.

A peculiarity in the itinerancy is, that while it develops all the powers, natural and acquired, which are in men who are industrious and faithful to their trust, it at the same time gives them a wider field for doing good. The prominent men in the Methodist ministry are more widely known by the people of the United States, and indeed in foreign lands, through the press, by the hearing of the ear, and by the seeing of the eye, than those of any other church; and the great majority of Methodist preachers, from the weakest to the ablest, reach, through the itinerancy, more people in a service of thirty or forty years than the ablest men in other churches. What a field for usefulness! What an encouragement to Methodist preachers to fail not in constantly doing their full and best work. Take the case of Mr. Spurgeon, of England, with all his marvellous success and the thousands of strangers who have attended his church in London; yet, is it not a fair inference that he would have done more good, have been the instrument of saving more souls, would have gained more influence and a greater reputation, if he had itinerated through the British Isles during the twenty-five years of his ministry?

Let our ministers be satisfied with the fact that under a closely-limited itinerancy a faithful man will have all the reputation and influence to which his abilities and piety entitle him.

Further, the plea that the more prominent churches

desire an extension of time, that their relative position of influence with other churches may be increased, is not true, nor is there anywhere heard, except under the direct influence of the pastors, a whisper in favor of a change.

Should the extension of time of service succeed, with the laity opposed to it, it may be profitable to forecast the probable influence of such extension on the ministry and the laity. If such extension should occur, one of two things will result: the laymen will be forced to demand protection at the hands of the bishops, and to secure it will control the purse. Such an extension of time would cause them to be more careful as to their pastors; it would increase the discrimination among the ministers, and absolute arrangements would then be made between the ministers and the laymen. Such extension would ultimately force many out of the Conferences from pure want of support. The result would be either a return to the two years' plan or an alteration of the law, by changing the provision which compels the bishop presiding to give an appointment to every minister in good standing, and confining his duties to an approval of the agreements made between the ministers and the churches. Taking, then, a broader view of the question of extension of time, will not the ministry come to see with the laity, that there is danger to the church in this effort of their brethren to gain and perpetuate their power by extending the time of service beyond three years?

Will they not see that injury to the Master's work will come?

First: By a reduction of the efficiency of the church.

Second: From the changed character of ministerial service and the lessened effectiveness of pulpit ministrations.

Third: From the difficulties it will create in the relations between the ministry and the people.

Fourth: In the injury it will inflict on many good men in the ministry, their wives and children, by forcing them out of the work.

COLORED STATEMENTS.

The *sixth* danger to the ministry arises from the temptation, for the supposed benefit of a church interest, to make statements orally, or by reports, or by communications, which are not strictly true, or in making false impressions by the suppression of the truth. Many ministers pride themselves on their ability as church beggars, but few preserve the respect of those who have been associated with them. Their methods are well understood, they need no exposition, and cannot be defended. The taking of collections, for church and denominational purposes, affords constant proof of the presence of the temptation to the ministers to mislead the people. By such conduct a doubt is cast upon the accuracy of financial statements coming from the pulpit, from the church boards, from the local and other charities; it affects the administration of every society of which the ministers have the management. Clerical solicitors who are permitted, under some kind of church authority, to make personal as well as public appeals for aid for perhaps worthy objects, are very liable to yield to this temptation.

The confidence of the church has been so often abused by this class that it may be a question if they do not more injury to the general interests of the church than good to specific cases. This subject is so delicate in its nature that perhaps the notice thus taken of it may suggest greater care in the future, both by pastors in charge, the representatives and agents of church societies, and travelling solicitors. The church cannot afford to have the integrity or the truthfulness of its ministry questioned. To have their proper influence, and to do the most good, and to preserve the confidence of the membership and the public, they must be above suspicion.

POWER OF THE PURSE.

The *seventh* danger to the ministry is found in the desire to retain the control of the purse of the church. This danger has hereinbefore been noticed. The ministers have now the practical control of all the financial interests of the church, from the power secured through the appointment of the stewards in the Quarterly Conferences up to and including the management of its educational and benevolent work and publishing interests. To retain such control is a strong temptation to frail humanity, but this is the policy of the ministerial party. The ministers should remember the teachings of history and the tendency of constitutional governments in this respect; they should know that the people in all countries, except in absolute monarchies, have demanded, fought for, and secured control of the purse, because there was no liberty or good government when the purse is controlled by or through the crown. The same wise and conservative provision prevails in our own country. All bills for expending money must originate in the popular assembly, the House of Representatives. In the great organizations of mankind, the exceptions to this most just principle are in the autocratic governments of the Old World, in the Roman Catholic, and in the Methodist Episcopal Church of the United States. If the experience of mankind teaches that the holding and exercise of this power over the purse tends to corrupt governments, how can the church escape? This power has injured it in the past, is corrupting it to-day, and will produce disaster in the future. The only safety lies in taking it out of the hands of the ministers. They hold it in violation of their calling. The vocation of the minister is to preach the everlasting truths of the gospel of Jesus Christ, not to use the money of the church for the power it gives in the world.

UNDUE INFLUENCE.

The *eighth* danger to the church arises from the temptation to the ministers in large cities and centres of population to secure undue influence over their brethren for their special purposes. It is well for the lovers of the Methodist Episcopal Church to look very closely at this source of danger.

History establishes two facts:

First: That the broadest-minded men and the ablest leaders of men are the products of the country as distinguished from cities or centres of large population.

Second: That rebellions, revolutions, and treason against governments have their origin and first life in cities or in densely-populated districts. If they are generated in the loneliness of the country, the heat of numbers is necessary to give them life and force.

The same laws apply to church governments; the dissatisfied, the disappointed, the unworthy, and the ambitious ministers can do but little in sowing seeds of disaffection towards the church or rebellion against it in country districts, villages, and in small towns. The large city offers greater facilities for combinations to carry out a settled plan, for in such places there are ministers of all grades. They frequently meet in bookrooms and in preachers' associations; they compare notes of their disappointments and bad treatment by bishops and elders, and work themselves up to believe that in place of being the most favored ministry of all the churches they are the most oppressed. Such men are in prime condition to be manipulated by the ministerial class party. They are duly trained upon the disposition of their votes for General Conference delegates, and are in a fit condition to do as their leaders bid them. They are in that frame of mind which enables leaders of revolutions and rebellions to handle unthinking masses: first, by making them believe that they are oppressed; and, second, that they will lead them into a land of promise.

The ministers and the laymen of the church outside of the great cities must carefully watch the utterances from preachers' meetings, the opinions of ministers who have long resided in cities, the teachings of the church papers, great or small, and all movements as to the polity of the church that originate in the cities in which are established book-rooms and church boards.

CONFERENCE AID SOCIETIES.

The *ninth* danger to the church is in the temptation to the ministers to interfere with the operation of the system of transfers, by reason of their personal interest in the various forms of aid and insurance societies that have grown up in the different Conferences.

It is acknowledged that these societies were the product of a necessity, that they have been very useful in relieving widows and orphans, that they have made many a minister's mind more easy as to the future of his family, that their help has come opportunely to meet the wants of families deprived of their head, and that in and of themselves they are most laudable institutions; but the question comes up: Have they any tendencies that are injurious to the church as a whole? The church, in view of what has already been written, will see, First, that they have a tendency to militate against the essence of the itinerancy in the needed facility of transferring ministers from one part of the work to another. In almost all of these societies the benefits are confined to the members of the Conference. To lose their interests in a society to which they may have contributed for a number of years, and in which they have acquired a valuable estate, is felt by the ministers to be a serious matter. The possibility of being transferred prevents many preachers from availing themselves of the benefits of such associations.

Second: That the interest in these societies increases the tendency to assert for an Annual Conference a separate existence and an entity involving rights and privileges inconsistent with the theory of the organization of the church, and thereby adds strength to the ministerial party, who are claiming specific rights as a class.

Thirdly: These societies have a tendency to separate the just claims of the ministry from the consciences and sympathies of the laity, and to thereby deprive the laymen of the benefits arising from a proper performance of all their duty to the church.

These societies have come into being because of a failure or the inability of the laymen to do their whole work as Christians. When the preachers are relieved from the care of all monetary affairs and are relegated to their proper work,—the care of the spiritual interests of their membership and of their fellow-beings,—and when the laymen are introduced as coequal legislators in the church, then it will be their duty to provide for the material interests of their pastors. A minister's church is one thing, a people's church another. When the latter comes, there should be no necessity for Preachers' Aid Societies.

It can scarcely be questioned that the knowledge

by the members of the church that the ministers and their families receive aid from the Chartered Fund, from the Book Concern, from Sustentation Funds, and from the different kinds of aid societies, reduces the collections for the worn out, the superannuated preachers and their families. Such a result is in accordance with experience and observation, and suggests some consideration of a collateral question.

ENDOWMENTS.

When are endowments or foundations for benevolent institutions desirable? A ready answer is, that they are necessary in all cases where a fixed income is required, and where the object is one that does not appeal directly to the sympathies of a church or of a people. Educational institutions, hospitals, asylums for the unfortunate, and such like interests, require endowments.

The benevolent and charitable institutions of a church are intended as much to develop the Christian characteristics of kindness, sympathy, and self-sacrifice in the contributors as to do good to others. Unless endowed institutions are of such public and general church interest as to secure a watchful care over them, they will fall into the control of a few, their offices will become sinecures, and the people will lose the benefit of the provisions made for their benefit. It was found a few years back, in London, that many endowed societies failed to perform their duties, and that the objects of some endowments had ceased to exist, and the interest of the fund was all used for the support of officials who did no work.

No endowments are requisite for the best work of benevolent and charitable institutions. When these are brought so close to the contributors that they know the work done by each institution, they will then feel that the responsibility is on them to supply their financial needs.

These suggestions refer properly to endowments for churches, for worn-out preachers, homes for the aged, for orphans, and for the many charities that abound in this country. They are made for the sake of showing that endowments tend to separate the beneficiaries from the people; and they are applicable to the different aid and relief funds in the Conferences. It may be well here to remind the laymen that the claim of the worn-out and superannuated preachers, their widows and orphans, for support is not based on charity, but is a matter of personal duty, as binding on them as the care of their own households. With the suggested changes in the church polity, the tax on the ministers to support these aid and insurance funds should not be required, and all temptations arising therefrom to interfere with the fixed policy of the church would be removed.

CONCLUSION.

The best correctives of the dangers to which the ministry is liable, through these several described temptations, will be applied when the legislation of the church is placed on a proper basis by the introduction of the laymen into all its councils, securing thereby the more perfect working of the itinerancy, by keeping the business of the Annual Conferences within proper limits, by more fully carrying out the policy of transfers, by a more constant introduction of the broad thoughts of the country to defeat the machinations of ambitious men in the cities, and by providing proper care for all who need help and comfort.

CHAPTER V.

The dangers that threaten the peace, purity, and prosperity of the Methodist Episcopal Church from an abuse of the representative power held by the Colored Conferences.

THE presence of the colored representatives in the last General Conference, their average intelligence, their liability to be used by shrewd ecclesiastical politicians (the ratio they held to the whole number of delegates being about one to nine),* must have suggested to thoughtful brethren a serious question of the wisdom of the continuance of the policy of the church as to them, both for their religious growth and welfare and for the peace, purity, and prosperity of the church. It is a broad question, and much may be said on both sides; time, it is trusted, will soon solve the problem.

A conclusive argument in favor of separation would be made if it could be satisfactorily proven that the

---

* The actual number of colored men elected as delegates to the last General Conference was forty-three (43), but there were forty-five (45) delegates from the Conferences known as colored. These delegates may be accepted as representatives of the colored people, and as expressing their opinions in all cases. There were also twenty-one delegates (twelve clerical and nine lay) from mixed Conferences.

connection as it now exists is injurious and demoralizing to both parties, if it could be shown that their presence is a danger and has a corrupting influence on the main body of the church, and that such separation could be made without injury to the colored man. There has been an unwillingness—a hesitation—on the part of the church to discuss this question, but the undoubted use that was made of the colored votes in the last General Conference to secure places was so patent to every careful observer that it cannot be kept down.

The ease with which the influence and votes of these innocent and generally very ignorant representatives were secured by those nearest to them, shows how great a danger there would be in the abuse of the confidence placed by them in their avowed friends. There is always danger in the presence, in a deliberative assembly, of any important number of members who are incapable of forming a correct opinion and are easily influenced. It is the object of ambitious leaders to win their support. If this is the case in the Assemblies, the Parliaments, the Congresses,—and there is acknowledged danger in it,—how much greater the danger in a Conference of the Methodist Episcopal Church, where extremely ignorant with a few educated men represent the large ratio of one in nine of its members. Does not this large proportion of ignorant men grade down the intelligence and wisdom of the whole body to a level too low for safety to, and for the guidance and control of, the interests of Christ's cause, as represented by the Methodist Episcopal Church? This danger is increased by the absence of any second house, on which all constitutionally governed countries depend for conservative influence. These are serious considerations. The members of the church must place a true value on the touching eloquence they have heard as to the great work among the negroes in the South; they must not give away their judgment to sentiment, they must consider the facts in the case and their influence on the church. There was a great deal of true sympathy, of a realization of Christian and patriotic duty, among the ministers and members of the Methodist Episcopal Church when, at the close of the war, there were found to be several millions of ignorant people cut loose from their old masters and made dependent on themselves, without the ability of their former owners to provide for them physical care and moral and religious teaching. In the demoralized condition of the South, there was an opening for the exercise of all such sympathy and Christian help, and these led the Methodist Episcopal Church to send many ministers, teachers, and large amounts of money to establish churches, schools, and colleges for their religious, intellectual, and physical benefit. Money was freely and often unwisely expended by the Missionary Society and by the Board of Church Extension, but more prudently by the Freedman's Aid Society. A great future was promised for the church; valuable properties were purchased in New Orleans, Richmond, Atlanta, and other places.

It was broadly and boastfully proclaimed that the Methodist Episcopal Church had gone to the South to remain, and plans for its religious conquests were ambitiously laid. One result was inevitable. Large crowds of colored people were gathered into the church. Wherever and whenever material help was promised, the colored people were at hand to receive it. The annual reports of the church showed a sudden and large increase of membership. Annual Conferences were established without regard to color, and their delegates were admitted in 1868 into the General Conference. Newspapers were published by order of the General Conference, and the losses paid by the willing North. What other results have been found? The general imprudence and lack of knowledge of the agents and ministers sent to the South have blocked up the way of the church. The immoral character and the dishonest practices of some inflicted disgrace on the church and cast a doubt on all. A majority of the good and able men sent to the South left as soon as they could be relieved from their duty. Men were brought into the ministry, both white and colored, who were totally and absolutely unfit. Yet they counted in numbers, and the church North was satisfied.

The church did not know the facts. It is said by those who know and judge impartially, that to-day there are but few men in any of the Southern colored and mixed Conferences who are fitted for their places, and that the colored members are still grossly immoral. These results might have been fairly anticipated from their circumstances and surroundings. The results of the work of the church in the South, as a whole, have not been satisfactory. The members are disappointed. These results come from the false theory on which such work was begun,—from an ignorance or a failure to comprehend the condition, wants, and character of the people of the South, both white and black, and as a sequence, from a failure to adapt the work to meet such conditions, wants, and character. There was too much zeal for the accompanying knowledge. The state of public feeling in the North at the time must be accepted as the apology for such errors of judgment. The mistakes have been committed, large amounts of money wasted, and the chances for usefulness of the church at many points largely diminished. It will be wisdom to hold the church to the present means of usefulness, and abandon hopes, plans, and ambitions which are now impossible.

There are important movements among the colored people that should be noted. All will remember the enthusiastic patriotism, civil and religious, which was to abolish all color lines and all laws that recognized black and white or their intermediate shades. Yet a law of nature, of race, and of common sense is asserting itself among the colored people in that they want to be separated from such close connection with the white man. They feel that there is an incongruity, an unfitness, a something that causes them to desire to be freed from his presence and government. They have but little respect for the whites who remain among them. It is a growing belief among the more intelligent colored people that their religious growth would be increased by their independence of the white church. So strong is this feeling, in certain places, that a secession from the Methodist Episcopal Church and the formation of independent Methodist Churches is seriously discussed. In obedience to this growing sentiment the General Conference in 1884 recognized the policy of basing membership of Annual Conferences on a color line.

An argument in favor of caution in treating this question may be drawn from the relation of the colored people to the interests of the country. The colored vote in the United States, due to a rapidly-increasing population (an increase said to be in excess of that of the white), is accepted as a source of danger in the future to this country. The present colored vote, as it has or has not had the privilege of free expression, has determined who should be President of the United States. The loss of this vote by suppression may place a party in power whose policy may be contrary to the wishes of a majority of the people. The use of a free expression, by a vote, may place an opposite party in power. If the colored people should increase in greater proportion than the white population, it would require but a few decades of years to give them the controlling influence in the Southern States. It may or may not be an idle fear, but wise men are looking at the question in sober earnestness. The granting of the ballot to this people was, and is, an acceptedly great strain on the national principle which gives every man a vote. The people have felt this, and yet thought it better to hold on to the principle, with the hope that increased intelligence, independence of thought and action, and development of manhood among the colored people would, with each passing year, lessen the strain. There are elements of strength and safety for the state in meeting danger from this direction that a church does not have.

The church, then, should be carefully guarded against danger arising from the presence of so large a colored membership through the use of its power in the General Conference.

The idea of separation for better work is not new among us. We have the German and Colored Conferences, and would have Scandinavian if there were enough Scandinavians. There is a law of association that is the best regulator of such questions. That a separation into Conferences on the color line will become general is inevitable.

The questions will come up before the General Conference to decide, whether the colored ministers can be so educated as to continue in the Methodist Episcopal Church without any serious danger to its interests; if not, the lesser must suffer, if suffering it would be, for the sake of the greater; or whether, when they are prepared, they will not do more good by being transferred to some branch of the African Methodist Episcopal Church.

There are the African, the Zion, and the Colored Methodist Episcopal Churches, which last was wisely set apart by the Southern Methodist Episcopal Church at the end of the war. They are all strong, aggressive, and independent churches. If the members of these churches could be united with the colored members of the Methodist Episcopal Church, they would make a membership of nearly one million of people. What an opportunity for usefulness to their race would be thus placed before them! It must be admitted that their continued connection with the Methodist Episcopal Church does not tend to promote their dependence upon themselves. Government aid makes a restless pauper class, church support has the same tendency. That the two races do not work well together, or rather that the colored churches do not prosper when intimately connected with white churches, is pretty well exemplified in the city of Philadelphia, where the only two colored churches, living side by side with the large white church membership of that city, had so dwindled in numbers and financial ability in 1884 that the Church Extension Society had practically to purchase two churches for their use, so that the colored brethren from the South might have a church home when they came to the General Conference. During the same time the African and the Zion Methodist Episcopal Churches have been very successful in that city, have done much good, have able bishops, leaders, and a respectable membership. On the one side there was dependency, and the other independency.

It is risking but little to assert that the number, character, and self-reliance of the members of the Colored Methodist Episcopal Church South are far greater and better than they would have been if their connection had continued with the old church.

A further thought deserves consideration at this point. If the colored members are to be continued in the church, or as long as such connection may last, would it not be to the interests of all parties to dissolve the Annual Conferences in which they are in a large majority, and form them into Mission Conferences, as they were prior to the General Conference of 1868, without a voting representation in the General Conference? By doing this the church would be saved from the low average grade of intelligence of the General Conference of 1884, caused by the presence of nearly forty of such representatives, and from the corrupting influences that were so palpable. The colored people would then understand that their connection was not permanent, but was in the line of educating them to take care of themselves. In the mean time the church could continue its good work in giving them the advantages of education, training in trades, and to the most promising, a fitting education for the ministry and learned professions.

The suggestions made hereinbefore as to the proper basis of representation in the General Conference, connected with that of the last paragraph, would reduce the number of delegates to the General Conference from the Colored Conferences, and thereby lessen the danger. It is important that this or some other protective plan should be adopted before the separation that is inevitable between the white and colored work takes place. No mere pride of numbers or prestige should have any influence to prevent the church from saying to the colored brethren, "Go in peace, and may the God of heaven protect and guide you," and with this benediction handing over to them all the churches, colleges, and property that have been accumulated for their use.

CHAPTER VI.

The influence of a thorough introduction of the laity, in every department of church legislation and work, on its prosperity; on the piety, effectiveness, and comfort of the ministry; and on the usefulness of the laity.

HAVING shown how an approximately fair representation of the laity may be engrafted on the present organization of the Methodist Episcopal Church with profit and advantage to all parties, and with injury to no person or interest, it is proper, before making a *résumé* of the whole discussion, to consider what the advantages are which will accrue to the church from the introduction of the laymen into all its councils. These advantages will be general to the church at large and personal as to the membership. Wherein the church will gain will be readily seen from a glance at the room there is for improvement between the interest the average member now takes in its progress and success and the abiding interest he might and should have. The following picture of the average lay member will be acknowledged as correct:

The lay brethren and sisters come into the church to find its services all they desire. The gospel preached meets their approbation; the helps in their Christian life are suited to their necessities; the spiritual part of the church is entirely satisfactory; they want nothing more; there can be nothing better. They find the offices filled by brethren in whom they have confidence; they learn of the Annual and General Conferences and of the different church boards, and discover that these are under the control of the ministry. They suppose this is all for the best; they acquiesce and finally approve; they feel that it removes all burdens from their shoulders, with a sprinkling of trust that the power would not be thus bestowed and so long held unless it met Divine approval, and that in some way it is a right thing for the church to be ruled by the ministers of Christ. They pay what they suppose is a fair proportion towards the support of their pastor and the elders. When the various benevolent causes are brought before them, without any specific knowledge of their merits and with almost no knowledge of their management, they contribute their share of the amount the preacher tells them is assessed upon their particular station or circuit. Their consciences are at ease when the salary of the preacher is not made up; they have given their share, and are willing the preacher should go around, cap in hand, to collect the balance. When the preacher in charge says there should be an addition to the church building, or a new one, or a parsonage, they say it is well enough if he can raise the money. He goes ahead, becomes the architect, constructor, and builder, and at the end finds the cost far beyond the estimate and the means of the members. This debt weighs upon the church for years, preacher after preacher tries to pay it, travelling beggars come to help, and in time at a great loss the debt may be paid; but the church has suffered in credit, in grace, and in numbers, for many are prevented from joining a debt-ridden, badly-managed society. The members feel no responsibility for the errors made; the preacher was the cause of the trouble, and it was his duty to see the society through its embarrassments. Meanwhile the laymen are having a good time; they sing, pray, and are free from personal censure. The church is governed by the ministry.

Yet with all this indifference, ignorance, and want of appreciation (the result of defective training), the work done by the Methodist Episcopal Church has been marvellous. It is no new thing on the earth for a people to be useful, either as slaves work under an overseer or serfs for a master, or as renters of ground for its owner; but in time they see their condition and revolt; the slaves and serfs demand freedom and the renters an interest in the ground they till. The Methodist laymen have not all been slumbering or living this life of indifference; with increasing intelligence and broader views of duty, they see the false position in which they have been so long placed, and they say to their rulers, "It is enough," and demand a change.

The question then comes with great force: Can the Methodist Episcopal Church afford to lose the active services of a laity who under the past unfavorable conditions have done so much for its advancement? Cannot the ministry see that the laity would have done much more for Christ's cause if a proper responsibility had been placed on them, and if they had been intelligently and actively engaged in serving it for the last twenty or more years? Is the love of power in the ministers of the church greater than their love for their fellow-beings whom Christ died to save? Is there any cause that can demand greater sacrifices of human ambition and desires on the part of the ministers than the cause of Christ? The grave question of lay representation in the Methodist Episcopal Church seems to depend on the answer to such questions,—the ministers should answer them as in the sight of God; if they will do this honestly and prayerfully, the Spirit of God will help them to overcome their infirmities.

It is more agreeable to write pleasant words than to expose error and wrong. To narrate wherein the laity may be made more useful to the church by their introduction, on an equality with the clergy, into all its councils would occupy more space than is available. Every member will see, almost instinctively, for he will at once compare what he has done with what he might have done. The first result would be a proper division of labor.

In the early church it was found that deacons had to be appointed to take care of the poor, that the apostles and disciples might be free to go into all countries and preach the gospel of their Lord Jesus Christ. There is as much need to-day as ever there was that the ministry should be free from worldly cares and responsibilities.

What nobler occupation is there for man than to be a faithful pastor of a loving people; devoting his whole time to persuading men to be reconciled with God, teaching the young, watching over them, bringing them into the church, building up the saints; showing by his own example the beauty and influence of a Christian life. These are the duties of a minister; in this service he reaps rich harvests and enjoys the happiness of knowing that he has done all that he could to make his fellow-men better and happier in this world, and to fit them for the enjoyment of an eternity of happiness in another state of existence. To be able to do this he must be relieved from anxiety as to a reasonable support; he must be freed from the care over church property, either in constructing, changing, or keeping it in repair; he must receive continued and hearty support from the laity in his endeavors to do work beyond the local church, whether such work is done by personal labors, by aid societies, or in other ways. Selfishness has no part in Christ's teachings; the best incentive to every minister is to be found in the words of the Master, "Freely ye have received, freely give." The second result of this division of labor would be that the laity would see that they have a work to do, that they must take charge of all the financial business of the church, must provide liberally for the support of its varied work; for in proportion as a church is progressive and aggressive will be the opening of places of usefulness, and the demand for money and men. The laymen must meet these wants so far as they can. It is a well-observed fact that providential openings and demands for money and men are made just as rapidly as the men are raised up for the special duty, and the laity have the ability and willingness to furnish the money to support them; when the progressive and aggressive spirit is at work, Providence will not let it fail for want of employment. It is idle to talk of awakening or arousing the laity to a full performance of their church duty unless the responsibility is clearly put upon them. If nature abhors a vacuum, man equally dislikes to work. It requires some stimulus to make men do their best; they do not willingly assume places of responsibility; they are always willing that others should do their work; but give them the incentive of a sacred duty and you may arouse a sleeping giant.

This division of labor, when every member of the church, the ministers and laity, are engaged at the parts of the great machine which they best understand, will secure the most perfect unification of the work, a blending of effort to a common end. In addition to the better support that will be secured to the ministers, and the better care of their widows and orphans, there would be developments in the way of church erection and improvement of church property little dreamt of by the most hopeful. The disgrace of begging old men, on the verge of the grave, to give to the church property which belongs to their heirs will be abandoned. The mission work of the church at home and abroad would receive a great impetus. Our colleges and academies would be more liberally endowed and better supported. The publishing interest of the church would be put on a proper basis, and all needed charitable institutions established and judiciously supported. The young and active men in the ministry will be freed from the efforts of their elders to make them humble, by keeping them down. The lists of the Conferences will be purged; there will not be so many dead-weights and hangers-on for the sake of place. The church councils will be purified; the seekers for office will be left at home; the church may lose some of its leaders, but the result will be that there will be an advance along the whole line, and in solid phalanx, shoulder to shoulder, the ministers and laymen will work to save fallen men. These results may not be at once secured; it may take time to educate the laymen to make good use of their privileges and to fully recognize their responsibilities. It is hard to throw off old habits; it takes time to educate the quondam slave to properly use his freedom, and the immigrant from foreign oppression to wisely use his rights and privileges as a citizen of the Republic.

The next point is the influence the introduction of the laymen into the councils of the church will have on their religious character. The first results would be increased self-respect and a development of the elements of manhood. No one holding a subordinate position can enjoy the feeling of independence of mind and action that comes with the responsibilities of life. The young wife and mother is a very different person from the girl in her father's house. The young man in charge of a business feels and acts very differently from what he did when a clerk or a subordinate partner. The enfranchised citizen has different thoughts and feelings from what he had when a slave or a serf. The right to deposit a vote, to be one of many to control the destinies of a nation, gives the young man very decided views of his responsibilities. When the laity feel that they are responsible to their Master for the management and working of their part of His church, they will then acquire a more intelligent understanding of its doctrines and of its form of government; they will learn to appreciate its peculiarities, and to know wherein its strength is to be found; they will become jealous of its good name and kindly critics of its defects, and will have for it a strong and deep attachment.

It will be said that these promised results partake of the character of hopeful anticipations without good grounds. It may be so, but if any such future is to come to the church at any time it must come in this way. The policy of suppression of the laity, with its results, has been partly described. The present state of inertia is its product. The members are alive to the interests of their individual societies; they rarely think or go beyond them.

The disfranchisement of the laity of the Methodist Episcopal Church—for this is the equivalent of the want of representation—has its injurious effects on the church in the lack of attachment to the church itself, as exhibited in the facility with which its members change their church relations, but more especially in the weak hold it has on the children of its members and young converts. Such attachment is largely due to home-training. If the parents have an intelligent love for the church, the children will inherit it. Disfranchised citizens have but little sympathy or attachment to their government; they and their children move into other countries and change their allegiance without a pang; having had no political influence or responsibility, they have no love for their rulers. The change is the more readily made when the country to which they migrate recognizes their manhood by giving them their full rights and places on them the responsibilities of citizenship. The laws of human nature work equally in both cases. The enfranchisement of the laity will produce as marked results as when the immigrant leaves a country where he was but little more than a chattel for one that clothes him with the dignity of citizenship. The change develops men; the new-made citizen will exert his best ability to justify the confidence thus bestowed on him.

The *first* result, then, of such enfranchisement will be seen in less wandering away from the church, and the Methodist Episcopal Church will cease to be the great reservoir from which so many churches draw for their ministers and for their members. While the church is willing to furnish a godly ministry to churches that have not enough religious vitality to supply their own pulpits, yet it would be better for all to remain in our own fold, where they can be better protected and educated in a true religious life. The effect of the leaven of Methodistic training and customs is to be seen in the increased spirituality and activity in good works of the other churches.

The *second* advantage will be that as the laity are brought to take more interest in the general church, to have a deeper interest in the spiritual welfare of their fellow-men, they will become more spiritually-minded, and be better men and women, with which graces will come enlarged influence for good in all the service of the church.

It may not be amiss just here to illustrate the ability of the laity to work successfully in Christ's cause, and its influence on them by the operations of the Woman's Foreign Missionary Society of the Methodist Episcopal Church. Its history is known to all. The causes of its marvellous success are generally understood; the hold it has on the people is so strong that the attempts in the last General Conference to secure its control by the Board of Missions failed through the decided expression of the lay members of that Conference, with the aid of many ministerial delegates. The success of that society, which has so won its way into the heart of the church and to a disciplinary recognition, proved the ability of the women of the church to originate, to manage, and secure the needed support of such an organization without the controlling aid of the ministers. It has been better managed, in many respects, than the General Board of Missions, and at the least possible expense. The women, with their intuitive knowledge and tact, have spread before their contributors, in the monthly visits of their admirable journal, the *Heathen Woman's Friend*, facts that give a clear understanding of the operations and expenditures of the society. While almost any intelligent member of the church can tell all about its missions and their success, it would be a rare thing to find any layman or woman who is as well posted in the work of the General Board. This illustration also proves the developing power of the responsibility thus assumed by the women,—a development in intelligence, wisdom, zeal, business aptitude, and, above all, in piety. The Woman's Foreign Missionary Society will have the direct effect of keeping many men and women in, and increasing their love for the church.

Again, there is a law of man's mental, moral, and religious nature that the ministers have not appreciated. It is found in the law of growth; the use of the muscles is necessary to physical development, of the mental faculties to mental power, of moral perception to correct action, of activity in good works to religious experience. Then, too, these uses must not only be in the proper line, but to the extent of one's capacity. The laity of the Methodist Episcopal Church feel that the time has come when, as grown men and women, they should be charged with the weighty responsibility of aiding in carrying on the great work of the church. They feel that they are competent to understand, to appreciate its wants, and to legislate concerning them; if this is refused and the intelligence and capacity of the laity are not employed, it is equivalent to saying that the Methodist Episcopal Church has no use for them, and bidding them go elsewhere for employment in Christ's vineyard. If this refusal is persisted in many must go, as many have in the past,—for to work is their duty, their life. The ministry should remember that while such men and women can live without the Methodist Episcopal Church, that church cannot afford to drive them away from its fold.

The true cause of the creation of the Woman's Home and Foreign Missionary Societies was this feeling by the women of the church, this sense of unrest because of their failure to be recognized or employed by the church in the line of missionary work, and to the extent of their capacity; it was a protest against the narrow policy and organization of the Missionary Board. In this work they have outstripped the laymen and, to their honor, pointed the way to work independently of ministerial control. It is the first duty of the church to keep its members actively engaged in labor in the cause of Christ. The church that most fully complies with this law of its existence will be the most useful and the most prosperous.

The influence of the form of government of the Methodist Episcopal Church on its members, in addition to the fact noticed of its tendency to narrow their interest to the society with which they are immediately connected, is to be found in the absence, omission, or non-recognition of the laity in the public exercises of the church, in the anniversaries of its societies and boards, and in public meetings of the general church,— the ministers naturally appropriating such representative places to themselves. These two exemplifications of the influence of priestly power on a people suggest very forcibly that there is an inherent defect in any organization that produces results that are contrary to all the accepted ideas of advance in the development of man, mentally and morally, and of the growth of the Christian Church. This fact was apparent at the recent centennial meetings. It might have been expected that such meetings would have been held without distinction between the ministers and the laity; that for once, and on so grand an occasion, the ministers would have dropped their leadership, and permitted a free expression by the laymen of their appreciation of the work done by Methodism in a hundred years. But caste is stronger than love of church, because it blinds the believer in caste to the virtues and rights of others. This failure to recognize the laity was evident at the centennial meetings in Baltimore, in December, 1884, where, out of twenty-four chosen topical speakers, there was but one layman, and he from the Church South, and of sixty-two platform speakers but eight laymen, the remaining seventy-seven being ministers in the various Methodist bodies.

How very remarkable this was will be better appreciated when the statement is made that Methodism includes nearly four millions of members and but some twenty thousand ministers, and that out of these millions of members but nine, or about one in some four hundred and forty thousand, were considered worthy of a place on the platform, or competent to point out the great achievements of the church in the past hundred years. As a result of this want of recognition, of this failure to make the laity bear their part of the remembrance, the contributions have failed to reach the desired and expected amounts. The heart of the laity was not in it.

There is another equally important thought connected with the influence of the polity of the church on the work of the laymen; it is found in their failure to bear their part of the public burdens of benevolence and influence that belong to all Christians. Christ has opened to His followers, for their profitable employment, many other kinds of service than those which peculiarly belong to individual churches or denominations. Many of these ways of doing good require the union of Christian laborers; they rise above the specialties of denominational interests to the level of a broad Christianity. In such work the Methodist and Catholic rarely appear, and when they are present, they have but little influence. The broad catholicism of the other Protestant Churches, and more especially those of the Presbyterian family, approves itself to the public mind, and gives them and their ministers an influence which cannot be reached by prolongation of term of service or such like remedies. It is said, in excuse for the failure of the Methodist laity to engage in such union of efforts, that they are engaged in their special church duties, and have not time for other religious employment; that other churches do not furnish so much work for their people, and, as they are fewer in numbers, they must join with others that they may have employment. There is some truth in these statements, but not enough to account for the shrinking and hesitation that Methodists show when invited to join others in religious labors of public interest.

The true reason for such failure to unite in the broader Christian work of the country is to be found in the fact that the Methodist people, like the Catholic, are educated to rely for everything in the way of leadership, or appearance in public, on their pastors. This failure of the Methodist laity to bear the full share of their religious duties to the public hinders their growth and the usefulness of the church. Methodist teaching and usages have not had a fair chance of making a proper impression on the members of other churches, or upon the public mind; its usefulness has been limited, and it has lost the benefits that would accrue to its members by their coming in contact with other Christians, and working in lines and ways outside of the regular church demands. This failure to bear their proper share of the public burdens has the effect of narrowing the minds of our members, and of lessening their knowledge of and interest in the general condition of humanity around them. The influence of a proper system of church government is seen in the greater freedom, already noticed, of the members of the Presbyterian family in engaging in all public movements for bettering the condition of humanity, in their liberty in expressing their opinions on all moral questions that may be before the public, and in all measures to sustain the majesty of the law, and to secure good rulers and magistrates. All this is the result of educating the individual to feel that he is an integral part of the Church of God, that he is responsible for its management, and must bear his share in all the duties of a Christian life. The equality of the teachers and rulers and members of the church, and the equality of their responsibility to God, is a noble basis for a Christian church. It is to be hoped that the members of the Methodist Episcopal Church may compare the results of its present polity with that of the Presbyterian

Churches, and see, in the comparison, good reason for a change.

That the result of these proposed changes in the polity of the church will be a spiritual benefit to the church as a body, to the ministry, and to the membership cannot be doubted.

CHAPTER VII.

Status of the clerical and lay members of the Methodist Episcopal Church on the question of increased lay representation.

IN the inauguration of any movement in the direction of an increased representation of the laity in the General Conference and their introduction into the Annual Conferences, it will be well to analyze the position of the ministry and of the laity on these propositions.

FIRST: The ministry. While the term "ministers" has been frequently used in this paper, it is expressly desired that it shall not be construed as intended to embrace all the ministers in the Methodist Episcopal Church. Nor can the opinions, desires, and intentions herein attributed to the laity be claimed as any more comprehensive. General terms have sometimes to be employed. It is acknowledged with thankfulness that the early ministers, who laid the foundation of the Methodist Episcopal Church broad and deep, were characterized by an almost romantic energy, self-denial, zeal, and earnestness, by great wisdom, religious fervor, and piety; and it does not derogate from their character and other virtues to say that among the ministry of to-day will be found their equals in all respects. Our honored fathers had their peculiar temptations arising from their relations to the church; the present race of ministers have other temptations as peculiar to them and to their relations to the church. It is also again stated that in no way has it been intended, in this essay, to cast odium upon any minister or the ministry, nor to question the sincerity of their motives. They have a right to express their opinions upon the church government, and to be respected therein, though others, as deeply devoted to the interests of the church, may think very differently, and see in the opinions of their brethren the seeds of danger to the church.

With these observations, the analysis of the position of the ministry on the question of lay representation shows, *First:* That there are many who thoroughly believe in giving the laymen full and equal representation in all the councils of the church, not only as a right, but as a wise and prudent policy. Their intimate relations with the laity have given them confidence in their piety, knowledge, and wisdom. They recognize the fact that the governments of nations and of the church are coming into the hands of the many. *Second:* That there are many who are indifferent to the question of lay representation, and are willing to accept any result. *Third:* Others, again, see no immediate reason for any change; they are submissive in spirit, yet would prefer the church to go on as it was when they were received into the fold. *Fourth:* There are those who are so conservative that any change is, in their opinion, questionable; they urge the let alone policy. If the world had depended on this sort of men, it would to-day be in the depths of barbarism. *Fifth:* There are others who, while unfavorable to the introduction of the laity, yet will not seriously oppose it because they consider it inevitable, and rather than see the church deeply agitated will yield the point.

These five classes comprise the great majority of the ministry, but there are three other classes.

The *Sixth*, while they believe the introduction of laymen is inevitable, yet will oppose it as long as possible, for the two reasons that they (the ministry) may have a longer lease of power and make the better bargain for themselves when the time of yielding comes. This class favor committees to examine and report at another General Conference, and approve all suggestions of delay.

The *Seventh* class are filled with the belief, as quoted by Macaulay, that, "while man made the House of Commons, yet God made the House of Lords," and that they are of this latter house, being divinely appointed to rule over God's church; that therefore any attempt to introduce the laity, and especially with power to judge of God's elect, would be scripturally wrong. These brethren abhor the idea of applying the principles of liberal governments to the church, and in this they have the example of many good men in the Catholic, Episcopal, and Lutheran Churches. The doctrine of their equality before God with the laity, they argue, applies to personal, not to church relations. They point to the success of the state churches of Europe and to the past history of Episcopal Methodism as illustrations of the necessity, for the success of a church, of there being absolute or largely controlling power in its ministry. These parties will fight the question to the bitter end; they, like the Bourbons, never learn.

The *Eighth* class sympathize with the latter brethren as to the necessity of such changes in the organic law of the church as will enable the members of an Annual Conference to control the *personnel* of its membership and in some way to control the appointments. To produce these results they keep clearly and distinctly in view, and as necessary steps, the lowering of the power of the bishops in the choice of the presiding elders, believing that, with these and some other organic changes, the power, the influence, and the position of the ministers will be increased.

The danger to the church at large comes from the three last-named classes, with the acquiescence of the fifth class. Rebellions and revolutions are rarely the spontaneous acts of a majority of a people; it is the sudden decided stand taken by the few who make an opinion for the public and precipitate rebellion. With such a variety of sentiment on this subject as thus stated among the ministers of the Methodist Episcopal Church, a few determined men can generally succeed in controlling the action of the majority.

SECOND: The laity. It may be profitable to analyze the position of the laity on this question. And, first of all, it may be said that wherever a people have from the origin of their nation or government been under an absolute rule, there has grown up with it a submissive spirit; any effort at change will be frowned down by the conservative among them. Such a people urge that "it is better to bear the ills they have than to fly to others they know not of," and through an education of years, they learn to accept their condition as from their Creator. They are trained to look to their rulers as their protectors, and to depend on them for advice and guidance in all the matters of life, and as to assuming any share of the responsibility of government they would hesitate, and rebellion would be resistance of God's holy appointed rulers. The same facts are true as to the influence of despotic churches. What Catholic would rise against the power of his church, against the Pope? or what Greek Christian against the power of the Czar, or Episcopalian against an edict of a Convention, or Methodist against the will of his minister? However, in time, with education, observation, and a knowledge of the way other people around them thrive and progress under self-rule, they make a first effort for freedom. It may fail or be partially successful, from the opposition of the laws of habit and training, of the powers of conservatism and the influence of their rulers; but when such a people appreciate their strength and the importance of the object to be gained, and make a united, determined effort, then their demands will be granted. This sketch of every year's history of the world presents a fair picture of the position of the laity of the Methodist Episcopal Church, with the same variety of parties, the same cast of characters which marks worldly examples.

There are many of the laymen who do not feel they

are ruled or oppressed because they have known nothing else. There are many who willingly avoid responsibilities; there are many who believe that their position in the church government should be changed, but fear lest agitation might do harm to the cause. There are many who sympathize deeply with the friends of lay representation, but feel they can do nothing to help it on. Again, there are many members who were disappointed that no favorable action was taken by the last General Conference. They feel there is no hope in waiting on the good sense of the ministry to act without pressure. They are now prepared to unite to educate, to gather in and crystallize the sentiment of the church, that the ministers may hereafter make no question as to their opinion or demand. The laity remember with great pleasure the labors of the worthy men, ministers and laymen, who for so many years gave their time and expended their money to educate the people up to the point that was gained in 1872,—the introduction of two lay representatives from each Annual Conference into the General Conference. Let the laity, with the aid of the broad-minded men in the ministry, again unite and a greater advance will be made.

CHAPTER VIII.

The laws of other churches respecting lay representation.

IT will be a matter of interest to the laity of the Methodist Episcopal Church to be reminded of the way other churches treat their members. The following memorandum has been prepared for this purpose. An examination of the polity of the different churches discloses several important facts.

FIRST: That in proportion as the churches are influenced by an inherited claim or relation to civil power, so is the power given to the ministry, and the converse, that as the churches are free from such influences so are the laity admitted to share in legislation. It will also be noticed that in all the churches except the Primitive Methodists of England and Ireland, and the Friends, the leaning is on the side of giving the advantage in representation to the ministry, evidently for the reason that the fact of a man being ordained as a minister gives him a right, *per se*, which the laymen has not, to legislate in the church councils. It is a relict of the claims of the ministers to govern the church that still lingers in the most democratic church governments.

SECOND: That the churches that most thoroughly ignore and exclude the laity from any participation in its government are the Roman Catholic and Greek Churches, the Church of England, and the Methodist Episcopal Church. This is a strange and unnatural union of names, and what is more to the point, and shows that something is defective in the Methodist Episcopal Church, is that the exclusive, aristocratic Church of England, with all its prelatical assumption of superiority, has been so impressed with the necessity of introducing its laymen into its councils, that its work as a church may be better done, that to secure this object the "Convocation" of Canterbury concluded, at its session in 1884, to form a "House of Laymen," the laymen to be appointed by the Diocesan Conferences of the province. Apropos of this, the last General Conference refused to permit laymen to be members of an Annual Conference, or to enlarge the number of lay representatives in the General Conference. How different the spirit and the intelligence which, under all its legal embarrassments, led the Church of England, apart from other reasons, to recognize the necessity of the presence of its laymen, that "its work as a church might be better done," with the narrow jealousy and petty action of the last General Conference in refusing the fullest use of the laity! The Methodist Episcopal Church has not the reasons for its unfortunate position that the Catholic Churches and the Church of England have for the power of the clergy and the ignoring of the laity. The Roman, Greek, and the English Churches constitute part of a government of which the Pope, the Czar, and the Queen of England are the heads. There may be some defence for these churches; there can be none for the Methodist Episcopal Church.

THIRD: The representative men of all the Protestant Churches recognize their lay members as conservative in their church action and policy. The Southern Methodist Episcopal Church, with the same general characteristics of doctrine and polity, acknowledges the advantage resulting from the presence of an equal number of lay and clerical members in their General Conferences, and an influential representation of laymen in their Annual Conferences. Their experience should be conclusive as to the proper policy of the church North, for they met the same practical difficulties in carrying out the plan that would be found in the Northern church.

MEMORANDUM.

Presbyterian Church.—Each church is governed by its session, consisting of the pastor and ruling elders elected by the members. Presbyteries are composed of the teaching elders of the churches in a given geographical district, together with one of the ruling elders elected for that purpose by the session from each church. Its duties are to inspect the personal conduct and pastoral labors of every minister within its bounds, and, when necessary, to admonish, suspend, or depose. It grants licenses to preach, gives certificates of character to those removing, and furnishes supplies.

The Synod is composed of the teaching elders and one ruling elder from each church of a larger district. The General Assembly, the supreme authority in ecclesiastical matters, embraces representatives, lay and clerical, in equal numbers. Voting is done *en masse.*

Protestant Episcopal Church.—Diocesan Conventions are composed of the clerical members of the diocese and of lay representatives from the churches.

Each parish is composed of a rector, vestry, and congregation. The vestries are elected by the congregation.

The General Convention is composed of two houses, —one of the bishops and the other of clerical and lay representatives chosen by the Diocesan Convention.

In all questions, when required by the clerical or lay representatives from any diocese, each order has one vote, and the majority of suffrages by dioceses is to be conclusive in each order, provided such majority comprehends a majority of the dioceses represented in that order.

Bishops are tried by a court of bishops. Ministers are received, tried, suspended, or dismissed by vote of the Standing Committee of each diocese, which is composed of the bishop, five clergymen, and five laymen. Bishops only can pronounce sentence on any clergyman, whether bishop, presbyter, or deacon.

Reformed Episcopal Church.—The form of government of this church differs from that of the Protestant Episcopal Church more in name than in fact, and in some respects it recognizes the equality of the laity more fully than the latter.

The Baptist Churches are independent; each one adopts its own articles of religion and form of government. Between the clergy and laity they recognize no other distinction than office.

German Reformed.—The government is Presbyterian. The elders and deacons are chosen by the members to form a Consistory. The Classis consists of ministers and one elder from each parish; it has charge of reception and trial of ministers. General Synod, the highest body, consists of ministers and elders chosen by the Classes.

Reformed Dutch.—Resembles the German Reformed in the principal features of government.

Church of God.—Supreme legislative body is, in its general council, "composed of the preachers in charge and the elders and deacons of each church, all of whom are elected by the elders."

Lutheran.—The Synods are made up of a minister and layman from each church. The lay representatives are elected by the council of the church, which is elected by the members. In the admission and trial of ministers the clergy and laity are on an equality.

Methodist Episcopal Church, South.—Annual Conferences are composed of travelling ministers and lay delegates, four of the latter (one of whom may be a local preacher) from every district.

The General Conference is composed of equal numbers of ministers and laymen.

Colored Methodist Episcopal Church, South.—Has the same general organization as the Southern Methodist Episcopal Church, with but one layman (one of whom may be a local preacher) from each district in the Annual Conference.

African Methodist Episcopal Church.—Provides for two lay representatives from each Annual Conference in the General Conference. The members composing the lay convention are chosen by vote of all the members of a district, voting *en masse.*

Friends.—There being no ordained ministers, the government is altogether in the hands of the members, male and female.

Moravian Brethren.—The American provincial Synod is composed of all ordained ministers and of lay delegates elected by the churches, and meets triennially.

Roman Catholic Church.—The power of government and of the purse are absolutely and exclusively in the hands of the clergy.

Church of England.—With the queen as its head, the management is in the hands of the state. The Convocation, a body to discuss church affairs, consists of two bodies, the one composed of archbishops and bishops, the other of representative clergymen chosen by the clergymen of each diocese.

Wesleyan Church.—The Conference, the legal hundred, is the highest legislative body. It consists of one hundred ministers, as provided for by Mr. Wesley in his Deed of Declaration of 1784, and by it this body was made perpetual.

In 1878 laymen were admitted to participate in all its proceedings except those affecting the ministerial office. The "Mixed Conference," so called, consists of an equal number of laymen and ministers.

New Connection Methodists.—The Conference is constituted on the representative system,—one layman and one minister from each church. Ministers are admitted and tried by both orders. Laymen have an equal voice with the clergy in the government of the church.

Primitive Methodists.—Their Conference is composed of one-third preachers and two-thirds laymen.

The Methodist Church of Canada.—Has equal representation in its councils. The lay members have no vote on ministerial character or on the admission of members to an Annual Conference.

Primitive Methodists of Ireland.—Ministers rank as laymen.

Australian Methodists.—Ministers and laymen unite in conducting the Annual Conference.

The Scotch Churches.—Are governed on the same principles as the Presbyterian Churches in the United States.

CHAPTER IX.

Résumé of the changes that are required in the organization and polity of the Methodist Episcopal Church to suit the present conditions that surround and affect its usefulness.

THE important question which now comes before the ministers and the members of the Methodist Episcopal Church is whether the time has not now come when its organization should be placed on a broader basis, in harmony with the teachings of Christ, the practices of the early church, and with the prevailing policy of the churches, both of this country and of England. A conscientious effort has been made plainly to show wherein the efficiency of the church may be injuriously affected, by a loss of its spiritual power, by the dangers that accompany marked success, by becoming a prey to political intrigue, by the ambition of its ministry to perpetuate their power in the church, by the ruinous tendency to the secularization of the ministry, and by the temptations peculiar to them as a class.

The preceding analysis has shown that the best results of church work are found in an union of responsibility and a wise division of labor; that the introduction of the laity into the councils of the Methodist Episcopal Church will tend to lessen the dangers that threaten its prosperity, and will give such councils increased wisdom and stability, will inspire the members with renewed zeal in the cause of Christ, and will react most favorably on the Christian character of the ministry and laity.

It has been acknowledged that the progress of the Methodist Episcopal Church has been so marked as to show, beyond doubt, that its organization was adapted to the spiritual wants, and to many of the conditions of the people of this country at an early date, and that it has been an instrument largely used by the Holy Spirit in the conversion of men. In the partial analysis made of the causes of such progress, its doctrines, methods, and organization were commented on, and the preservation of the itinerancy insisted upon, as being the best means of reaching with the gospel the largest number of people; of giving them the highest average of service; of securing the more regular employment and the better support of its ministry; of developing their abilities; of opening the widest field for their personal and pulpit influence; of aiding them in godly living; and of building up the general church of Jesus Christ.

BASIS OF ARGUMENT.

The controlling principles which influenced this investigation of the polity of the church and determined its conclusions were:

First: The assumption that the whole membership, including the ministry, is answerable to God for the use of the trust given them in the form of the Methodist Episcopal Church.

Secondly: That this responsibility is measured by its

present conditions and future possibilities, and that the members cannot avoid this responsibility by continuing to depute such care to the ministry.

It is their personal duty to secure this proper care of the church in the most practicable way, and with the least friction in disturbing existing habits and usages.

Thirdly: That the ultimate test of any and all proposed changes in the polity of the church should be their influence on its efficiency.

The changes in its organization suggested in this paper to carry out such principles are based on four other principles which are practicable and protective in their nature:

First: Equal representation and equal powers of the ministry and the laity in the two councils of the church,—the General and Annual Conferences.

Second: That the representation of the itinerant ministry in the General Conference should be confined to the effective itinerant men.

Third: That membership in an Annual Conference, on the clerical side, should be limited to the effective travelling ministry.

Fourth: That the ministers should be aided by all the conditions that will enable them to do the best work, and be protected from the presence of inducements which tempt them to give up the active ministry or lead them into secular pursuits.

That the proposed changes may be fully considered by the church it is asked that they be tried by answers to the following leading questions,—many others will suggest themselves to the reader:

First: What influence would these proposed changes in the polity of the church have on the work of the itinerancy, the attachment of the ministry and membership, and on its efficiency?

Second: Would not the efficiency of the church be increased by recognizing the truth, "That the membership of the church is entitled, either collectively in the persons of its members, or representatively, by persons chosen out of or by the laity, to a voice or influence in all the acts of legislation and government?" (Principles, New Connection.)

The changes suggested come under their respective headings, and are as follows:

FOR THE GENERAL CONFERENCE.

I. To provide that the General Conference shall be composed of equal numbers of lay and clerical delegates, chosen as may be provided by the Discipline.

II. That the basis of representation of both orders should be the numbers of the members, and in case where the members of an Annual Conference are not equal to the number required for the election of two delegates (one clerical and one lay), then the members of adjoining Conferences may be united to secure such representation.

III. That the representation should be confined, on the clerical side, to effective ministers attached to Annual Conferences engaged in the travelling ministry, including presiding elders, ministers in charge of stations, circuits, and missions, and presidents and professors of the theological schools, universities, colleges, and schools under the care of the Methodist Episcopal Church, and secretaries of the American and State Bible Societies when Methodist preachers.

IV. That no minister acting as a representative in a General Conference should be eligible to the office of bishop, nor to any of the official positions which are filled by election by such Conference.

V. That the clerical and lay members shall have an equal right to call for a vote by orders, or to sit apart in the discussion of any question before taking a vote, a majority of both orders being required to carry a measure when a separate vote is taken.

VI. That in the election of the bishops, and of all other officials, a separate vote shall be taken by orders, or, in other words, it shall require a majority of both orders, clerical and lay, voting separately and apart, to elect a bishop or any person to any official place.

VII. In place of the last two articles, preference should be given to the recommendation that provision should be made for the creation of two bodies in the General Conference, the one composed of the clerical, the other of the lay, delegates, that all acts of the Conference should require the assent of a majority of both houses; that the choice of bishops should be protected by requiring a vote of more than only a majority of both houses; that other officials might be elected by a simple majority.

VIII. The General Conference should meet but once in six years.

FOR THE ANNUAL CONFERENCE.

I. To provide for either equal (clerical and lay) representation or, if more convenient and practicable, for not less than six lay representatives from each district in each Annual Conference.

II. That the ministerial membership of the Annual Conferences shall be confined to the presiding elders and the ministers in charge of circuits and stations; presidents and professors in the theological schools, universities, colleges, and schools under the care of the church, secretaries of the church boards, clerical editors of the church newspapers and reviews, and secretaries of the American or State Bible Societies. That the preachers holding superannuated or supernumerary relations, or appointments other than as above specified, may be members of an Annual Conference, without right to vote, or to be delegates to a General Conference, until such time when the General Conference shall provide that membership in the Annual Conferences shall be confined, as originally designed, to the active ministry, all other ministers holding their relation to the church at large, and amenable for their conduct to the Annual Conference in whose bounds they reside.

III. That the clerical and lay members shall have the same right to a separate vote, and shall be governed in all respects by the same powers as in the General Conference, except that they shall meet as one body.

IV. That both orders shall have equal authority to perform all duties committed to the Annual Conference, such as the admission of men into the ministry, the trial and suspension or expulsion of a minister, the granting and fixing of superannuated, supernumerary, or local relations, with or without the consent of the persons so affected.

CHANGES IN THE RESTRICTIVE RULES.

I. To provide that all changes in the " Restrictive Rules" shall require the assent of three-fourths of the clerical and lay members voting separately in the Annual Conferences, to be followed by two-thirds of the same orders voting separately in the General Conference.

QUARTERLY CONFERENCE.

I. That the Quarterly Conference shall consist of a fixed number of members of a station or circuit, to be chosen by the members of the church every two, three, or four years, or a certain portion every year, and shall be charged generally with the performance of the duties now assigned to that body.

ELECTORAL COLLEGE.

I. That the delegates to the lay convention shall be elected by the members of each station or circuit in such way and at such times as may be determined.

GENERAL CONFERENCE BOARDS AND SOCIETIES.

The principle of equality in representation between the ministry and laity to be introduced into all parts of the management of the different boards of the charitable societies of the church. The secretaries to be elected by the boards of managers of each interest.

The changes as to the publishing interests and the colored membership being mixed questions of polity and policy, may be safely left to the discretion of the General Conference when composed of an equal number of lay and clerical representatives.

The following suggestions embrace the results of the discussion of these questions:

THE PUBLISHING INTERESTS.

That the policy of the church as to the extent of its publishing interests should be determined by three principles,—*First:* The propriety and duty of the church to provide for its people the Bible and the literature needed to explain and enforce its teachings. *Second:* That the extent of such service should be limited or measured by the willingness or ability of private enterprise to supply the same. *Third:* That there should be a constant effort made to keep down the capital employed and the real estate held by, and the number of agents and employés of, the Book Concerns.

The committee appointed to look after these interests should consist of three-fourths laymen and one-fourth ministers, and be authorized to elect the editors of the papers, the reviews, and the Book Agents in New York and Cincinnati.

THE COLORED CONFERENCES.

The setting apart of the colored members of the church into an independent organization will be wise and prudent, because, *First:* It will be for their religious and moral benefit, and, *Second:* It will remove a temptation to white church politicians to misuse and abuse their confidence. *Third:* It will increase the average intelligence of our General Conferences. *Fourth:* It will add to the stability of the church by lessening the ability to change imprudently the "Restrictive Rules." *Fifth:* It will be but anticipating the inevitable. An absolute separation will be better than a gradual falling off of the better class of the colored people.

With a further suggestion, that until such separation takes place all the Annual Conferences, composed wholly of colored ministers or of some fixed proportion of mixed colors, shall be made Mission Conferences with or without right of representation, but without the right to vote.

The changes herein recommended, it will be observed, affect only the polity of the church. Are they not based on sound principles? Will they not tend to protect the church against the temptation now felt by the ministry, to abuse their power, by dividing such power with the laity? In place of the tendency in the ministry to form a class interest, will not such changes secure the more perfect union of the ministry and the laity in the work of the church? Will not the division of labor between them be a benefit physically and spiritually to the ministers, and spiritually to the laymen? Will they not tend to lessen the temptations that now have so much influence on the ministers, leading them to become dissatisfied with the itinerancy of the church, ambitious for place and honor, and seekers for place, drawing them into a condition of mind where they become a prey to the more skilful handlers of men, and thereby lose their peace of mind and usefulness? Will not such changes develop legislative and executive talent in the laity, the men and women of the church? Does not the success of the Woman's Foreign Missionary Society give promise of coming results when the responsibility of caring for the charities of the church is fully placed upon the laity?

Finally, will not the influence of such changes as are herein proposed in the polity of the church tend to more fully develop the itinerancy, in its best directions, to increase the love and zeal of the ministers and laymen, and, by these and other results, greatly increase the efficiency of the Methodist Episcopal Church?

HARMONY.

In the minds of many the questions will be suggested, What effect will an effort to secure these changes have on the harmony of the church? Will it in any way tend to create disturbance, divisions, unkind and unchristian feeling? Will such an effort, even for a time, thwart the work of grace or impede its growth and usefulness? These are important questions, and merit a candid answer. It is acknowledged that all reforms create some friction. It is the will of the Creator of all things that by means of storms, with their destructive effects, nature may find in the desired equilibrium, peace. Just wars may exist, with their loss of life and property, to settle contests between great principles, and thereby produce more lasting peace and increased prosperity. The responsibility is with those who stand in the way of the liberalization of governments. Habits and customs in church government, as well as in state and in social life, resist changes. An extreme conservatism, for fear that one change may beget another, retards progress; violent or radical changes in governments require strong efforts, and take time for a people to adapt themselves thereto. In the present case there should be no violent disturbances or disagreements. The proposed changes are not radical, because they are in the line of the development of the constitutions of all governments both of church and state, and they harmonize with the prevailing thought of the American people. The tendencies of legislation in the church are in that direction; the critical point in the Methodist Episcopal Church was passed in 1872, in the admission of lay representatives to the General Conference. The presence of the laity on committees in the Annual Conferences has been a preparatory step. Such changes would be a natural outgrowth of the church towards greater usefulness,—a recognition of a necessity to keep pace with the demands of the cause. The Methodist Episcopal Church, in taking this long step forward, would be brought up to the level of the other Protestant Churches by a recognition of the rights of nearly two millions of her people.

In the face of such results, who would create trouble in the church? Who would be the disunionist? Who would hinder the work of grace, or impede the growth and usefulness of Methodism? It would not be the laymen.

It is hoped that these pages will be of service to those in the ministry who in all good conscience have been led astray in their judgment, by opening their eyes to the existence of facts and dangers they may not have seen. To the younger and abler men in the ministry it opens a way by which they may escape from the humiliating process of being kept down and hampered in their usefulness to make way for unacceptable men who demand the best places. To the active ministers it secures the honors as well as the burdens, and places them on a higher platform, by recognizing, as the sainted Lybrand did in declining office, that the work of the pastor was the highest on earth. To many of the ministry who are fast going down towards that dread level of unacceptability, the proposed changes offer the full benefits of the policy of transfers which will add years to their usefulness. To all the ministry these changes offer greater influence in the church, better care of themselves and families, and relief from worldly anxieties.

The arguments and recommendations in the foregoing pages are submitted to the ministry and laity for their examination and concluding judgment. They are believed to be in the line of true progress, and are protective of all interests. The abiding desire has been to suggest such changes as will tend, First: To keep the church close to her spiritual work. Second: To keep the ministry free from the temptations of the world, the flesh, and the devil. Third: To develop the laity by placing upon them their full share of the work of the church.

It may and probably will be that all the suggestions may not receive approval: some may think that while these may be good in themselves, yet that it is best to make haste slowly, to take one step at a time; that the securing equal representation in the General Conference and satisfactory representation in the Annual Conferences will suffice for the first step; that the other suggestions may be acted upon as stronger indications of danger to the church may appear from any source. This course may be prudent. But this exposition shows the necessity of the first step. Let that be taken. How can it be secured? Let not the laity flinch from looking the question in the face and meeting the facts. The analysis hereinbefore given of the position of both orders, clerical and lay, on this question is a fair exposition of the difficulties the laity will meet. Every thoughtful member will see that the attention of the laymen must be thoroughly aroused to appreciate the justice and importance of securing proper representation in the church councils.

The duty of all those in either the clerical or lay ranks, who believe in the necessity of some changes, is to agitate the question of lay representation. Agitation is a necessity in securing any great reform; a grand necessity in all struggles with power. It is not revolutionary, but conservative. Let such members who believe in the laity talk with their fellow-members about it; let them examine it, analyze it, try it in every shape; argue on the merits of the proposed changes for the good they will effect, and for the dangers they will prevent to the most cherished interests of the church, and as the best provision against the tyrannical use of the " power to command." Let there be consultation and comparison of views in groups of the laymen. Let the laity hold church meetings, circuit meetings, district meetings, meetings at Annual Conferences, Church Congresses, to discuss this question of representation. Let the lay conventions of 1887 and 1888 express themselves strongly, and see to it that no one is elected to the next General Conference who will not support such changes. Let there be a representative mass-meeting held in New York City, in May, 1888, to express to the General Conference the judgment of the church, as to the necessity of such changes. There will then be no miserable quibbles about the wishes of the laity, and no more committees appointed. Let the laymen, with the more intelligent of the ministry who sympathize with them, prepare proper papers covering the changes they deem best for the church and cause, and demand their passage by the General Conference and in time by the Annual Conferences. The result may be surely foreseen. The policy of right, of justice, of equality, of prudence, of wisdom, of religion, will be successful, and the Methodist Episcopal Church will, free from the tutelage of the schoolmasters, enter upon the work of its manhood.

While the criticisms and suggestions herein made have had a more direct application to the present and near future interests of the church, yet in a broader sense they are as strongly directed to the prosperity of the church in that farther future which is looming up before the thoughtful; for that time when the church shall become so large in numbers, and so extended and varied in her interests, as to have grown beyond the adaptability of the present machinery of its organization. Such a time is in the future; it may be forty, fifty, or more years before it comes. The nearer it is (and the time of its coming will depend on the faithfulness of its members, lay and clerical), the more necessity is there for preparing the constituency of the church to meet their future responsibilities, by now broadening the basis of the polity of the church, through the introduction of equal lay representation in all its councils and Conferences. If this is done, eternity alone can write the history of the Methodist Episcopal Church, or tell of its usefulness as one of the means used by the great Head of the church to save fallen men.

THE END.

www.ingramcontent.com/pod-product-compliance
Lightning Source LLC
Chambersburg PA
CBHW022043230426
43672CB00008B/1059